Program Planning Guide

Level II

EMC Publishing

ST. PAUL • LOS ANGELES • INDIANAPOLIS

Level II Program Planning Guide

Care has been taken to verify the accuracy of information presented in this book. However, the authors, editors, and publisher cannot accept responsibility for Web, e-mail, newsgroup, or chat room subject matter or content, or for consequences from application of the information in this book, and make no warranty, expressed or implied, with respect to its content.

Trademarks: Some of the product names and company names included in this book have been used for identification purposes only and may be trademarks or registered trade names of their respective manufacturers and sellers. The authors, editors, and publisher disclaim any affiliation, association, or connection with, or sponsorship or endorsement by, such owners.

ISBN 978-0-82193-081-6

© 2009 by EMC Publishing, LLC
875 Montreal Way
St. Paul, MN 55102
E-mail: educate@emcp.com
Web site: www.emcschool.com

Printed in the United States of America

18 17 16 15 14 13 12 11 10 09   1 2 3 4 5 6 7 8 9 10

CONTENTS

Unit 4

Unit 5

Unit 6

Unit 7

Introduction

This comprehensive *Program Planning Guide* serves as a road map to the entire *Mirrors & Windows: Connecting with Literature* program. It lists all the components available for each lesson in the textbook and offers options that help you address your own curriculum needs, student requirements, and schedules. This integrated approach makes it easy to incorporate language arts skills such as reading, vocabulary, critical thinking, and media literacy into each lesson.

To help you meet the diverse needs of your students, the *Mirrors & Windows* program offers a wealth of material—much more than you can teach in one school year. As a result, one challenge you will face is identifying the resources that are best suited to your particular situation. The *Program Planning Guide* offers several tools to help you meet that challenge.

The guide begins with a Core Standards-Based Selections chart outlining a basic course of study for teaching the critical skills covered in formal language arts assessments. If you start your curriculum planning with this chart, you will know that you are teaching the key material your students need for success.

Three types of lesson plans are provided in the body of this guide:
- **Unit introduction** plans allow you to plan your teaching of each unit and introduce the unit.
- **Selection** plans include one or more selections, plus workshops and special features that are grouped with those selections.
- **End-of-unit workshop** plans cover the workshops that appear at the end of each unit.

The lesson plans begin with pacing, selection details (if applicable), and objectives. They are then broken into the following categories to provide easy identification of the information you need: Plan, Preview and Motivate, Teach, Differentiate Instruction, Review and Extend, and Assess. Each plan lists all the supplemental resources that support the lesson:
- *Meeting the Standards* activities and quizzes
- *Differentiated Instruction* lessons
- *Exceeding the Standards* lessons
- *Assessment Guide* tests and exams
- Technology Tools: *EMC Launchpad, Annotated Teacher's Edition on CD, Interactive Student Text on CD, ExamView® Assessment Suite on CD, ETS Online Criterion-Based Essay Grader (Grades 9–12), Visual Teaching Package, EMC Audio Library, EMC E-Library,* and **mirrorsandwindows.com**

Additional planning materials appear in your *Annotated Teacher's Edition*. The Visual Planning Guide at the start of each unit presents a quick view of the supplemental materials available for each selection. The Scope and Sequence Guide provides a breakdown of the apparatus for each selection, including literary elements, reading level and reading skills, cross-curricular connections, and the *Mirrors & Windows* theme.

The **E-Lesson Planner** packages the entire *Mirrors & Windows* program, including the lesson plans, in one easy-to-use calendar resource. With the *E-Lesson Planner*, you can link directly to activities listed in the lesson plans, search complete versions of all teacher resources, download correlated state standards directly into your lesson plans, customize lesson plans and save links to your own resources and lessons, drag and drop prepared lesson plans into a calendar, display multiple course plans on one calendar, and export completed course plans to your Microsoft® Outlook® calendar.

Mirrors & Windows
Core Standards-Based Selections
Level II (Grade 7)

The selections and workshops listed here represent the core course of study students need to master critical skills that appear on formal assessments. To ensure standards coverage, students who are having difficulty may concentrate on only these selections and workshops. Students on and above grade level may read more selections.

Unit	Selections	Literary Skill	Reading / Informational Skills	Pacing Regular Schedule	Pacing Block Schedule
UNIT 1 FICTION **Grammar & Style Workshops:** Pronoun-Antecedent Agreement; Nominative & Objective Pronouns **Vocabulary & Spelling Workshop:** Denotation & Connotation **Writing Workshop:** Expository Writing: Responding to a Short Story **Speaking & Listening Workshop:** Giving & Actively Listening to Oral Summaries	After Twenty Years	Plot	Analyzing Cause and Effect	3 days	1.5 days
	The Portrait	Plot	Analyzing Cause and Effect	2 days	1 day
	A Day's Wait	Conflict	Drawing Conclusions	2 days	1 day
	Informational Text: Mars Climate Orbiter Team Finds Likely Cause of Loss		Drawing Conclusions		
	The War of the Wall	Dialect	Analyzing Cause and Effect	2 days	1 day
	Comparing Literature: Rikki-Tikki-Tavi / The Green Mamba	Personification, Conflict, Setting	Making Predictions, Asking Questions, Making Inferences	4 days	2 days

Unit	Selections	Literary Skill	Reading / Informational Skills	Pacing	
				Regular Schedule	Block Schedule
UNIT 2 FICTION **Grammar & Style Workshops:** Comma Use; Independent & Dependent Clauses; Consistent Verb Tense **Vocabulary & Spelling Workshop:** Prefixes, Roots, & Suffixes **Writing Workshop:** Narrative Writing: Writing a Short Story **Speaking & Listening Workshop:** Giving & Actively Listening to Literary Presentations	The Scholarship Jacket	Theme	Using Context Clues	3 days	1.5 days
	Amigo Brothers	Point of View	Drawing Conclusions, Clarifying Information	3 days	1.5 days
	Informational Text: *from* The Greatest: Muhammad Ali	Point of View	Drawing Conclusions	3 days	1.5 days
	Four Skinny Trees	Description	Identifying Main Idea	1 day	0.5 day
	The White Umbrella	Mood	Comparing and Contrasting	2 days	1 day
	Seventh Grade	Character	Identifying Sequence of Events	2 days	1 day
UNIT 3 NONFICTION **Grammar & Style Workshops:** Sentence Types; Fragments & Run-on Sentences **Vocabulary & Spelling Workshop:** Greek, Latin, & Anglo-Saxon Roots **Writing Workshop:** Expository Writing: Cause-and-Effect Essay **Speaking & Listening Workshop:** Giving & Actively Listening to Informative Presentations	Elizabeth I	Biography	Distinguishing Fact from Opinion	4 days	2 days
	Primary Source Connection: *from* Queen Elizabeth's Speech to Her Last Parliament et al.	Meter, Setting	Analyzing the Effects of Form on Content		
	Names/Nombres	Personal Essay	Identifying Author's Purpose	3 days	1.5 days
	The Eternal Frontier	Persuasive Essay	Analyzing Main Idea & Supporting Details	2 days	1 day
	Fish Cheeks	Sensory Details	Analyzing Text Structure	1 day	0.5 day

Unit	Selections	Literary Skill	Reading / Informational Skills	Pacing	
				Regular Schedule	Block Schedule
UNIT 4 NONFICTION **Grammar & Style Workshops:** Simple & Compound Subjects **Writing Workshop:** Descriptive Writing: Descriptive Essay **Viewing Workshop:** Critical Viewing	*from* The Sibley Guide to Birds	Visual Media	Drawing Conclusions	2 days	1 day
	Informational Text: *from* Wild Turkey	Anecdote	Analyzing Author's Perspective		
	Ships in the Desert	Analogy	Analyzing Main Idea & Supporting Details	3 days	1.5 days
	Informational Text: I Am a Native of North America	Analogy, Description	Comparing & Contrasting		
	Comparing Literature: Mute Dancers: How to Watch a Hummingbird / The Hummingbird That Lived Through Winter	Description	Asking Questions	3 days	1.5 days
UNIT 5 POETRY **Grammar & Style Workshops:** Personal & Possessive Pronouns; Nouns: Proper, Plural, Possessive, & Collective; Reflexive & Intensive Pronouns **Vocabulary & Spelling Workshop:** Synonyms & Antonyms **Writing Workshop:** Expository Writing: Compare-and-Contrast Essay **Speaking & Listening Workshop:** Giving & Actively Listening to Expository Presentations	Gold	Imagery	Identifying Main Idea	1 day	0.5 day
	Feel Like a Bird	Metaphor & Simile	Monitoring Comprehension	2 days	1 day
	Father William	Rhyme	Analyzing the Effects of Form on Meaning	2 days	1 day
	Blackberry Eating	Alliteration	Identifying Author's Perspective	1 day	0.5 day
	The Village Blacksmith	Rhythm	Using Context Clues, Evaluating Author's Purpose	2 days	1 day
	Mother to Son	Repetition	Identifying Main Idea	2 days	1 day
	Under the Apple Tree	Free Verse	Identifying Multiple Levels of Meaning	2 days	1 day
	Informational Text: *from* The Botany of Desire	Tone, Voice	Visualizing		

Unit	Selections	Literary Skill	Reading / Informational Skills	Pacing	
				Regular Schedule	Block Schedule
UNIT 6 POETRY	Once by the Pacific	Symbolism	Analyzing Text Organization	1 day	0.5 day
Grammar & Style Workshops: Simple, Compound, Complex, & Compound-Complex Sentences; Simple, Complete, & Compound Predicates	Comparing Literature: Annabel Lee / The Highwayman	Narrative Poem	Making Predictions, Identifying Cause & Effect	1 day	0.5 day
	The Filling Station	Tone	Identifying Main Idea	1 day	0.5 day
	Name Giveaway	Lyric Poetry	Analyzing Text Organization	2 days	1 day
Vocabulary & Spelling Workshop: Figurative Language	Ancestors	Author's Purpose	Analyzing Main Idea & Supporting Details	1 day	0.5 day
Writing Workshop: Narrative Writing: Personal Narrative	I'm Nobody	Hyperbole	Summarizing	1 day	0.5 day
Speaking & Listening Workshop: Giving & Actively Listening to Narrative Presentations	The Pasture	Mood	Asking Questions	1 day	0.5 day
UNIT 7 DRAMA	A Defenseless Creature	Drama	Identifying Cause and Effect	3 days	1.5 days
Grammar & Style Workshop: Verbals: Participles, Gerunds, & Infinitives	A Christmas Carol: Scrooge and Marley, Act 1	Plot	Drawing Conclusions	3 days	1.5 days
Vocabulary & Spelling Workshop: Using Dictionaries & Thesauruses	Informational Text: *from* What Jane Austen Ate and Charles Dickens Knew	Mood	Identifying Main Idea		
Writing Workshop: Persuasive Writing: Persuasive Essay	A Christmas Carol: Scrooge and Marley, Act 2	Theme, Setting	Monitoring Comprehension, Making Inferences	4 days	2 days
Speaking & Listening Workshop: Giving & Actively Listening to Persuasive Presentations	Primary Source: *from* A Christmas Carol	Characterization	Asking Questions, Summarizing		

Unit	Selections	Literary Skill	Reading / Informational Skills	Pacing	
				Regular Schedule	Block Schedule
UNIT 8 FOLK LITERATURE	Persephone and Demeter	Myth	Monitoring Comprehension	2 days	1 day
Grammar & Style Workshops: Misplaced Modifiers; Dangling Modifiers	Eshu	Folk Tale	Identifying the Main Idea	1 day	0.5 day
	The Secret Name of Ra	Motivation	Analyzing Cause & Effect	3 days	1.5 days
Vocabulary & Spelling Workshop: Homographs, Homophones, & Homonyms	Literature Connection: *from* Akhenaton's Hymn to the Sun	Sensory Details, Metaphor	Asking Questions, Paraphrasing		
Writing Workshop: Expository Writing: Research Report	Phaëthon, Son of Apollo	Allegory	Drawing Conclusions	2 days	1 day
Speaking & Listening Workshop: Giving & Actively Listening to Research Presentations	Comparing Literature: The Instruction of Indra / Such Perfection	Symbolism	Monitoring Comprehension, Comparing	3 days	1.5 days
	Aunty Misery	Simile	Analyzing Cause and Effect	1 day	0.5 day
	How the Snake Got Poison	Folk Tale	Identifying the Main Idea	1 day	0.5 day

Name: _____ Date: _____

Reading Log

Week of _____

Date	Title	Author	Pages Read		Summary/ Reactions
			From	**To**	

Total number of pages read this week: _____

Genres read this week (circle):

Fiction   Nonfiction   Poetry   Drama   Folk Literature

Name: _____ Date: _____

Communicating in a Pair Group: Self-Evaluation

Communicating with another person is a two-way street: it involves both listening carefully and speaking clearly. Being an effective communicator when interacting with another person includes

- making eye contact and maintaining a relaxed posture
- providing feedback as you listen
- not interrupting
- rephrasing what the speaker says to show you understand
- controlling your emotions
- distinguishing between facts and opinions

Evaluating Pair-Group Communication—Self-Evaluation

Use the scales on this page to analyze and rate yourself on the items below. Place a check mark at the point on the scale that you feel corresponds to your number for each item. Then give yourself an overall score for how well you communicated with your partner and write a short evaluation. Suggest ways that you could improve your communication skills.

I made eye contact and maintained a relaxed posture.

_____
4   3   2   1   0

I provided feedback as I listened.

_____
4   3   2   1   0

I did not interrupt.

_____
4   3   2   1   0

I rephrased what my partner said to show that I understood.

_____
4   3   2   1   0

I controlled my emotions.

_____
4   3   2   1   0

I backed up facts with details from the text and gave my opinions.

_____
4   3   2   1   0

Overall score _____

Suggestions for improvement

_____

_____

_____

Name: _____ Date: _____

Communicating in a Pair Group: Peer-Evaluation

Communicating with another person is a two-way street: it involves both listening carefully and speaking clearly. Being an effective communicator when interacting with another person includes
- making eye contact and maintaining a relaxed posture
- providing feedback as you listen
- not interrupting
- rephrasing what the speaker says to show you understand
- controlling your emotions
- distinguishing between facts and opinions

Evaluating Pair-Group Communication—Peer Evaluation

Use the scales on this page to analyze and rate your partner on the items below. Place a check mark at the point on the scale that you feel corresponds to your partner's number for each item. Then give your partner an overall score for how well your partner communicated and write a short evaluation. Suggest ways that your partner could improve his or her communication skills.

My partner made eye contact and maintained a relaxed posture.

_____
4   3   2   1   0

My partner provided feedback as he/she listened.

_____
4   3   2   1   0

My partner did not interrupt.

_____
4   3   2   1   0

My partner rephrased what I said to show that she/he understood.

_____
4   3   2   1   0

My partner controlled his/her emotions.

_____
4   3   2   1   0

My partner backed up facts with details from the text and gave her/his opinions.

_____
4   3   2   1   0

Overall score _____

Suggestions for improvement

_____

_____

_____

Name: _____ Date: _____

Communicating in a Small Group

Communicating in a small group requires all the elements of effective communication between two people. But when you're working with a small group, it's also necessary to observe some other guidelines. These include
- respecting group norms, or rules that govern behavior for group members
- understanding group roles (possible group roles: reader, timekeeper, recorder, summarizer, foreperson)
- taking turns
- helping to create a positive climate
- establishing group goals

Evaluating Small-Group Communication

Use the scales on this page to analyze and rate your group on the items below. Place a check mark at the point on the scale that you feel corresponds to your group's number for each item. Then give your group an overall score for how well it communicated and write a short evaluation. Suggest ways your group could improve its communication.

Group members understand and respect group norms.

_____
4   3   2   1   0

Group members understand group roles.

_____
4   3   2   1   0

Group members take turns participating.

_____
4   3   2   1   0

Group members help to create a positive climate.

_____
4   3   2   1   0

Group members work together to establish group goals.

_____
4   3   2   1   0

Overall score _____

Suggestions for improvement

_____

_____

_____

_____

_____

_____

_____

Name: _____ Date: _____

Communicating in a Large Group

Large groups require many of the same skills you use in a small group. However, large groups also require special communication skills. Some of these skills are

- sharing group roles so everyone can participate
- focusing on key relationships and finding key people to lead the group
- emphasizing group identity and setting reachable goals
- standing up when presenting
- avoiding "groupthink," the pressure to conform
- taking responsibility and helping each other finish tasks

Evaluating Large-Group Communication

Use the scales on this page to analyze and rate your group on items below. Place a check mark at the point on the scale that you feel corresponds to your group's number for each item. Then give your group an overall score for how well members communicated with each other and write a short evaluation. Suggest ways that your group could improve its communication skills.

Group members shared roles so everyone could participate.
_____
4   3   2   1   0

Group members focused on key relationships and key people who could lead our group.
_____
4   3   2   1   0

Group members emphasized a group identity and set reachable goals.
_____
4   3   2   1   0

Group members stood up when making presentations.
_____
4   3   2   1   0

Group members stated their opinions and were not pressured to conform.
_____
4   3   2   1   0

Group members took responsibility for completing the assignment and helped each other finish tasks.
_____
4   3   2   1   0

Overall score _____
Suggestions for improvement

_____

_____

_____

_____

Name: _____ Date: _____

Asking Questions: Questioning Skills

Knowing the most effective ways to ask and answer questions in a group can help you become a great communicator. Here are some guidelines to remember when asking questions.

- Wait to be recognized.
- Make your questions short, clear, and direct.
- Don't debate or argue with the speaker.
- Don't take too much of others' time.
- Don't give a speech yourself.

Evaluating Questioning Skills

Use the scales on this page to analyze and rate your abilities for the items below. Place a check mark at the point on the scale that you feel corresponds to your number for each item. Then give yourself an overall score for how well you asked questions, and write a short evaluation of your abilities, suggesting ways you could improve your communication skills.

I waited to be recognized.

_____

4   3   2   1   0

I asked short, clear, and direct questions.

_____

4   3   2   1   0

I did not debate or argue with the speaker.

_____

4   3   2   1   0

I did not take too much time asking questions.

_____

4   3   2   1   0

I did not give a speech when I asked a question.

_____

4   3   2   1   0

Overall score _____

Suggestions for improvement

_____

_____

_____

_____

_____

_____

_____

Name: _____ Date: _____

Answering Questions: Answering Skills

Here are some guidelines to remember when answering questions.
- Be prepared for a question-and-answer period.
- Be patient.
- Make your answers clear, short, and direct.
- Rephrase difficult questions.
- Be courteous.
- Try to handle difficult members of the audience gracefully.

Evaluating Answering Skills

Use the scales on this page to analyze and rate your abilities on the items below. Place a check mark at the point on the scale that you feel corresponds to your number for each item. Then give yourself an overall score for how well you answered questions, and write a short evaluation of your abilities, suggesting ways you could improve your communication skills.

I was prepared for a question-and-answer period.

_____
4   3   2   1   0

I was patient.

_____
4   3   2   1   0

I gave clear, short, and direct answers.

_____
4   3   2   1   0

I rephrased difficult questions.

_____
4   3   2   1   0

I was courteous.

_____
4   3   2   1   0

I handled difficult members of the audience gracefully.

_____
4   3   2   1   0

Overall score _____

Suggestions for improvement

_____

_____

_____

_____

LESSON PLAN

Name: _____ Date: _____

Unit 1 Fiction Opener, p. 2

Pacing
- **Regular Schedule:** 1 day
- **Block Schedule:** 0.5 day

Objectives
Studying this lesson will enable students to
- connect the themes expressed in the selections to their own lives and to the world around them

- identify common forms of fiction, including the short story
- understand common elements of fiction, including plot, character, setting, and mood
- understand variations of literary forms and authors' use of language to develop forms

---

Plan the Unit
Use the following resources to plan instruction for this unit:
_____ Unit 1 Visual Planning Guide: Unit-Based Resources, *ATE*, pp. 2A–2B
_____ Unit 1 Visual Planning Guide: Lesson-by-Lesson Resources, *ATE*, pp. 2C–2D
_____ Unit 1 Scope & Sequence Guide, *ATE*, pp. 2E–2H
_____ Unit 1 Building Vocabulary, *ATE*, pp. 2I–2J
_____ Launch the Unit, *ATE*, p. 2

Teach the Unit Opener
Choose from the following resources to teach the unit opener:
_____ Unit 1 Overview, *SE/ATE*, pp. 2–3
_____ Introduction to Fiction, *SE/ATE*, pp. 4–5
_____ Fiction Study Guide: Introduction, *Meeting the Standards Unit 1*, p. 1
_____ Fiction Study Guide: Master Vocabulary List, *Meeting the Standards Unit 1*, p. 18

Differentiate Instruction
Consider the following alternative teaching options to differentiate instruction:
_____ English Language Learning, *ATE*, p. 5

Extend the Unit
Choose from the following resources to extend the unit:
_____ For Your Reading List, *SE/ATE*, p. 125
_____ Unit 1, *Exceeding the Standards: Grammar & Style*, pp. 1–19
_____ Lifelong Learning: The Definition of Character: Part 1, *Exceeding the Standards: Special Topics*, pp. 1–2
_____ Media Literacy: Internet Research, *Exceeding the Standards: Special Topics*, pp. 3–5
_____ Unit 1, *Exceeding the Standards: Vocabulary & Spelling*, pp. 1–12

Assess

Administer the following assessment tool(s):

_____ Formative Surveys 1 and 2, *Assessment Guide*, pp. 3–20

_____ Reading Fluency Assessments, Passages 1 and 2, *Assessment Guide*, pp. 293–294

_____ Unit 1 Exam, *Assessment Guide*, pp. 253–256

Technology Tools

Enhance the lesson with interactive activities offered in these technology supplements:

- EMC Launchpad
- Annotated Teacher's Edition on CD
- Interactive Student Text on CD
- Exam*View*® Assessment Suite on CD
- Visual Teaching Package
- ETS Online Criterion-Based Essay Grader (Grades 9–12)
- EMC Audio Library
- EMC E-Library
- **mirrorsandwindows.com**

Name: _____ Date: _____

Literary Element: Understanding Plot, p. 6

After Twenty Years, p. 9

Vocabulary & Spelling Workshop: Denotation and Connotation, p. 16

Guided Reading: Reading Model
- **Reading Level:** Moderate
- **Difficulty Consideration:** Vocabulary and irony
- **Ease Factor:** Plot twist

Pacing
- **Regular Schedule:** 3 days
- **Block Schedule:** 1.5 days

Objectives

Studying this lesson will enable students to
- use reading skills such as analyzing cause and effect
- define plot and analyze how characters deal with conflict
- describe the literary accomplishments of O. Henry
- appreciate a story that has an unexpected twist

Before Reading

Teach the Feature(s)

Select from the following resources to teach the feature(s):

_____ Literary Element: Understanding Plot, *SE/ATE*, pp. 6–7

_____ Differentiated Instruction: Reading Proficiency, *ATE*, p. 7

_____ Fiction Study Guide: Understanding Plot and Applying Plot to the Selections, *Meeting the Standards Unit 1*, pp. 2–5

Preview and Motivate

Choose from the following materials to preview the lesson and motivate your students:

_____ Fiction Reading Model, *SE/ATE*, p. 8

_____ Before Reading, *SE/ATE*, p. 9

_____ How to Read Fiction, *Meeting the Standards Unit 1*, pp. 19–21

_____ Build Background, *Meeting the Standards Unit 1*, p. 22

During Reading

Teach the Selection(s)

Choose from the following resources to teach the selection(s):

_____ During Reading, *SE/ATE*, pp. 10–14

_____ Reading Skills: Draw Conclusions, *ATE*, p. 13

_____ Build Vocabulary: Using Context Clues with Outdated Words, *Meeting the Standards Unit 1*, p. 23

Differentiate Instruction

Consider the following alternative teaching options to differentiate instruction:

_____ Reading Proficiency, *ATE*, pp. 11, 12
_____ Kinesthetic Learning, *ATE*, p. 11
_____ English Language Learning, *ATE*, p. 12
_____ Enrichment, *ATE*, p. 14
_____ Author/Genre Study: Hallmark of O. Henry's Short Stories, *Differentiated Instruction for Advanced Students*, pp. 1–3
_____ Analyze Cause and Effect, *Differentiated Instruction for English Language Learners*, pp. 1–9

After Reading

Review and Extend

Use the following materials to review and extend the lesson:

_____ After Reading, *SE/ATE*, p.15
_____ Analyze Literature: Plot Diagrams, *Meeting the Standards Unit 1*, p. 25
_____ Extend the Text: Make Predictions, *Meeting the Standards Unit 1*, p. 26
_____ Collaborative Learning: Investigate Police Work, *Exceeding the Standards: Extension Activities*, pp. 1–2
_____ Summarize Fiction, *Exceeding the Standards: Literature & Reading*, pp. 1–2
_____ Narrative Writing: Tell About a Person in Action, *Exceeding the Standards: Writing*, pp. 1–6

Teach the Workshop

Select from the following materials to teach the workshop:

_____ Vocabulary & Spelling: Denotation and Connotation, *SE/ATE*, p. 16
_____ Language Arts Handbook 2.6, Understanding Denotation and Connotation, *SE/ATE*, pp. 842–843
_____ Denotation and Connotation, *Exceeding the Standards: Vocabulary & Spelling*, pp. 43–44

Assess

Administer the following assessment tool(s):

_____ Selection Quiz, *Meeting the Standards Unit 1*, p. 27
_____ Lesson Test, *Assessment Guide*, pp. 23–25

Technology Tools

Enhance the lesson with interactive activities offered in these technology supplements:

- EMC Launchpad
- Annotated Teacher's Edition on CD
- Interactive Student Text on CD
- *ExamView®* Assessment Suite on CD
- Visual Teaching Package
- ETS Online Criterion-Based Essay Grader (Grades 9–12)
- EMC Audio Library
- EMC E-Library
- **mirrorsandwindows.com**

LESSON PLAN

Name: _____   Date: _____

Literary Element: Understanding Characters, p. 17

The 11:59 / *from* A Long Hard Journey: The Story of the Pullman Porter, p. 18

Guided Reading: Reading Model
- **Reading Level:** Moderate
- **Difficulty Consideration:** Foreshadowing
- **Ease Factor:** Short sentences and paragraphs

Pacing
- **Regular Schedule:** 4 days
- **Block Schedule:** 2 days

Objectives
Studying this lesson will enable students to
- use reading skills such as note taking
- analyze character development
- explore the work of Patricia and Frederick McKissack
- synthesize content from different texts to appreciate a story about a dedicated worker

---

Before Reading

Teach the Feature(s)
Select from the following resources to teach the feature(s):
_____ Literary Element: Understanding Characters, *SE/ATE*, p. 17
_____ Fiction Study Guide: Understanding Characters and Applying Characters to the Selections, *Meeting the Standards Unit 1*, pp. 6–8

Preview and Motivate
Choose from the following materials to preview the lesson and motivate your students:
_____ Fiction Reading Model, *SE/ATE*, p. 8
_____ Before Reading, *SE/ATE*, p. 18
_____ Build Background: History Connection, *Meeting the Standards Unit 1*, p. 29
_____ Literary Connection: Metaphor, *Meeting the Standards Unit 1*, p. 30
_____ Preview Vocabulary, *Meeting the Standards Unit 1*, p. 31

During Reading

Teach the Selection(s)
Choose from the following resources to teach the selection(s):
_____ During Reading, *SE/ATE*, pp. 19–25
_____ Vocabulary Skills: Dialect, *ATE*, p. 21
_____ Grammar Skills: Capitalization, *ATE*, p. 23
_____ Vocabulary Skills: Context Clues, *ATE*, p. 24
_____ Speaking & Listening Skills: Evaluate and Interpret Literary Texts, *ATE*, p. 25
_____ Informational Text Connection: from *A Long Hard Journey: The Story of the Pullman Porter*, *SE/ATE*, pp. 26–27
_____ Research Skills: Generate Questions for Research Topics, *ATE*, p. 27
_____ Analyze Literature: Supernatural Fiction, *Meeting the Standards Unit 1*, p. 32

Differentiate Instruction

Consider the following alternative teaching options to differentiate instruction:

_____ English Language Learning, *ATE*, pp. 20, 26
_____ Enrichment, *ATE*, p. 20
_____ Kinesthetic Learning, *ATE*, p. 22
_____ Visual Learning, *ATE*, p. 22
_____ Reading Strategies and Skills Practice: Make Predictions, *Differentiated Instruction for Developing Readers*, p. 1

After Reading

Review and Extend

Use the following materials to review and extend the lesson:

_____ After Reading, *SE/ATE*, pp.25, 28
_____ Use Reading Strategies: Make Connections, *Meeting the Standards Unit 1*, p. 33
_____ Analyze Literature: Fiction vs. Nonfiction, *Meeting the Standards Unit 1*, p. 34
_____ Subjects and Predicates: The Basic Building Blocks in a Sentence, *Exceeding the Standards: Grammar & Style*, pp. 7–9

Assess

Administer the following assessment tool(s):

_____ Selection Quiz, *Meeting the Standards Unit 1,* p. 35
_____ Lesson Test, *Assessment Guide*, p. 26

Technology Tools

Enhance the lesson with interactive activities offered in these technology supplements:

- EMC Launchpad
- Annotated Teacher's Edition on CD
- Interactive Student Text on CD
- Exam*View*® Assessment Suite on CD
- Visual Teaching Package
- ETS Online Criterion-Based Essay Grader (Grades 9–12)
- EMC Audio Library
- EMC E-Library
- **mirrorsandwindows.com**

LESSON PLAN

Name: _____ Date: _____

Literary Element: Understanding Setting, p. 29

The Inn of Lost Time, p. 30

Grammar & Style Workshop: Subject-Verb Agreement, p. 48

Guided Reading: Reading Model
- **Reading Level:** Challenging
- **Difficulty Consideration:** Length, frame story, and vocabulary
- **Ease Factor:** Interesting plot

Pacing
- **Regular Schedule:** 3 days
- **Block Schedule:** 1.5 days

Objectives
Studying this lesson will enable students to
- use reading skills such as analyzing sequence of events
- explain how setting affects plot
- sample the historical fiction of Lensey Namioka
- appreciate a story with an interplay of mystery, confusion, and truth

---

Before Reading

Teach the Feature(s)
Select from the following resources to teach the feature(s):
____   Literary Element: Understanding Setting, *SE/ATE*, p. 29
____   Fiction Study Guide: Understanding Setting and Applying Setting to the Selections, *Meeting the Standards Unit 1*, pp. 9–10

Preview and Motivate
Choose from the following materials to preview the lesson and motivate your students:
____   Fiction Reading Model, *SE/ATE*, p. 8
____   Before Reading, *SE/ATE*, p. 30
____   Build Background: Prior Knowledge, *Meeting the Standards Unit 1*, p. 36
____   Vocabulary: Word Families, *Meeting the Standards Unit 1*, p. 37

During Reading

Teach the Selection(s)
Choose from the following resources to teach the selection(s):
____   During Reading, *SE/ATE*, pp. 31–46
____   Reading Skills: Monitor Comprehension, *ATE*, p. 33
____   Writing Skills: Sensory Details, *ATE*, p. 35
____   Vocabulary Skills: Log of New Words, *ATE*, p. 37
____   Reading Skills: Skim and Scan, *ATE*, p. 39
____   Speaking & Listening Skills: Oral Interpretation, *ATE*, p. 41
____   Vocabulary Skills: Irregular Verbs, *ATE*, p. 42
____   Vocabulary Skills: Prefixes and Suffixes, *ATE*, p. 43
____   Grammar Skills: Commas with Introductory Phrases, *ATE*, p. 45
____   Analyze Literature: Setting, *Meeting the Standards Unit 1*, p. 39
____   Mythology Connection, *Meeting the Standards Unit 1*, p. 40

Differentiate Instruction

Consider the following alternative teaching options to differentiate instruction:

_____ Reading Proficiency, *ATE*, p. 32
_____ English Language Learning, *ATE*, p. 32
_____ Enrichment, *ATE*, pp. 34, 38, 44
_____ Visual Learning, *ATE*, pp. 36, 40

After Reading

Review and Extend

Use the following materials to review and extend the lesson:

_____ After Reading, *SE/ATE*, p. 47
_____ Use Reading Strategies: Make Connections, *Meeting the Standards Unit 1*, p. 41
_____ Literary Connection: Setting, *Meeting the Standards Unit 1*, p. 42
_____ The Sentence and Its Functions, *Exceeding the Standards: Grammar & Style*, pp. 1–6

Teach the Workshop(s)

Select from the following resources to teach the workshop(s):

_____ Grammar & Style: Subject-Verb Agreement, *SE/ATE*, p. 48
_____ Language Arts Handbook Section 3.7, Agreement, *SE/ATE*, pp. 862–863
_____ Subject and Verb Agreement, *Exceeding the Standards: Grammar & Style*, pp. 75–78

Assess

Administer the following assessment tool(s):

_____ Selection Quiz, *Meeting the Standards Unit 1*, p. 43
_____ Lesson Test, *Assessment Guide*, p. 29

Technology Tools

Enhance the lesson with interactive activities offered in these technology supplements:

- EMC Launchpad
- Annotated Teacher's Edition on CD
- Interactive Student Text on CD
- Exam*View*® Assessment Suite on CD
- Visual Teaching Package
- ETS Online Criterion-Based Essay Grader (Grades 9–12)
- EMC Audio Library
- EMC E-Library
- **mirrorsandwindows.com**

LESSON PLAN

Name: _____ Date: _____

The Portrait, p. 49

Grammar & Style Workshop: Pronoun-Antecedent Agreement, p. 56

Directed Reading
- **Reading Level:** Moderate
- **Difficulty Consideration:** Abrupt shifts and lack of speaker tags
- **Ease Factor:** Suspense

Pacing
- **Regular Schedule:** 2 days
- **Block Schedule:** 1 day

Objectives
Studying this lesson will enable students to
- use reading skills such as analyzing cause and effect
- define plot and recognize the elements of plot in the selection
- describe literary accomplishments of Tomás Rivera and explain the influence of Mexican-American culture on his writing
- appreciate a story of loss and remembrance

Before Reading

Preview and Motivate
Choose from the following materials to preview the lesson and motivate your students:
_____ Before Reading, *SE/ATE*, p. 49
_____ Build Background: Share a Photo, *Meeting the Standards Unit 1*, p. 45
_____ Build Background: Interview a Grandparent, *Meeting the Standards Unit 1*, p. 46

During Reading

Teach the Selection(s)
Choose from the following resources to teach the selection(s):
_____ During Reading, *SE/ATE*, pp. 50–54
_____ Grammar Skills: Sentence Fragments, *ATE*, p. 53
_____ Writing Skills: Sensory Details, *ATE*, p. 35
_____ Analyze Language: Euphemisms, *Meeting the Standards Unit 1*, p. 47
_____ Analyze Literature: Narrator, *Meeting the Standards Unit 1*, p. 48
_____ Creative Writing: Speaker Tags, *Meeting the Standards Unit 1*, p. 50

Differentiate Instruction
Consider the following alternative teaching options to differentiate instruction:
_____ Reading Proficiency, *ATE*, pp. 51, 54
_____ Auditory Learning, *ATE*, p. 51
_____ English Language Learning, *ATE*, p. 52
_____ Enrichment, *ATE*, pp. 52, 54
_____ Cultural Context Project: Mexican American Culture, *Differentiated Instruction for Advanced Students*, p. 4

After Reading

Review and Extend
Use the following materials to review and extend the lesson:

____ After Reading, *SE/ATE*, p. 55

____ Make Connections, *Meeting the Standards Unit 1*, p. 51

____ Lifelong Learning: Research the Internet, *Exceeding the Standards: Extension Activities*, p. 3

Teach the Workshop(s)
Select from the following materials to teach the workshop(s):

____ Grammar & Style: Pronoun-Antecedent Agreement, *SE/ATE*, p. 56

____ Language Arts Handbook 3.4, Pronouns, *SE/ATE*, pp. 856–858

____ Pronouns and Antecedents, *Exceeding the Standards: Grammar & Style*, pp. 37–39

Assess
Administer the following assessment tool(s):

____ Selection Quiz, *Meeting the Standards Unit 1*, p. 52

____ Lesson Test, *Assessment Guide*, p. 32

Technology Tools

Enhance the lesson with interactive activities offered in these technology supplements:

- EMC Launchpad
- Annotated Teacher's Edition on CD
- Interactive Student Text on CD
- Exam*View*® Assessment Suite on CD
- Visual Teaching Package
- ETS Online Criterion-Based Essay Grader (Grades 9–12)
- EMC Audio Library
- EMC E-Library
- **mirrorsandwindows.com**

Name: _____ Date: _____

A Day's Wait / Mars Climate Orbiter Team Finds Likely Cause of Loss, p. 57

Directed Reading
- **Reading Level:** Moderate
- **Difficulty Consideration:** Dialogue
- **Ease Factor:** Length

Pacing
- **Regular Schedule:** 2 days
- **Block Schedule:** 1 day

Objectives
Studying this lesson will enable students to
- use reading skills such as drawing conclusions
- analyze how characters deal with conflict
- describe the writing style of Ernest Hemingway and explain how his work influenced other writers
- appreciate a story about courage

Before Reading

Preview and Motivate
Choose from the following materials to preview the lesson and motivate your students:
_____ Before Reading, *SE/ATE*, p. 57
_____ Build Background: Math Connection, *Meeting the Standards Unit 1*, p. 54

During Reading

Teach the Selection(s)
Choose from the following resources to teach the selection(s):
_____ During Reading, *SE/ATE*, pp. 58–60
_____ Informational Text Connection: "Mars Climate Orbiter Team Finds Likely Cause of Loss," *ATE*, pp. 61–62
_____ Research Skills: Compare Sources, *ATE*, p. 61
_____ Literary Connection: Style, *Meeting the Standards Unit 1*, p. 55

Differentiate Instruction
Consider the following alternative teaching options to differentiate instruction:
_____ Reading Proficiency, *ATE*, p. 59
_____ English Language Learning, *ATE*, p. 59
_____ Enrichment, *ATE*, p. 60
_____ Draw Conclusions, *Differentiated Instruction for English Language Learners*, p. 10

After Reading

Review and Extend
Use the following materials to review and extend the lesson:
_____ After Reading, *SE/ATE*, pp. 60, 62
_____ Use Reading Strategies: Make Connections, *Meeting the Standards Unit 1*, p. 57

Assess

Administer the following assessment tool(s):

_____ Selection Quiz, *Meeting the Standards Unit 1*, p. 58

_____ Lesson Test, *Assessment Guide*, p. 34

Technology Tools

Enhance the lesson with interactive activities offered in these technology supplements:

- EMC Launchpad
- Annotated Teacher's Edition on CD
- Interactive Student Text on CD
- Exam*View*® Assessment Suite on CD
- Visual Teaching Package
- ETS Online Criterion-Based Essay Grader (Grades 9–12)
- EMC Audio Library
- EMC E-Library
- **mirrorsandwindows.com**

Name: _____ Date: _____

The War of the Wall, p. 63

Grammar & Style Workshop: Nominative and Objective Pronouns, p. 72

Directed Reading
- **Reading Level:** Moderate
- **Difficulty Consideration:** Historical references
- **Ease Factor:** Interesting plot

Pacing
- **Regular Schedule:** 2 days
- **Block Schedule:** 1 day

Objectives

Studying this lesson will enable students to
- use reading skills such as analyzing cause and effect
- define dialect and recognize its effect in the selection
- describe the literary accomplishments of Toni Cade Bambara and explain how the Harlem community influenced her writing
- appreciate a story of creativity and discovery

Before Reading

Preview and Motivate

Choose from the following materials to preview the lesson and motivate your students:

_____ Before Reading, *SE/ATE*, p. 63

_____ Build Background: Historical Context, *Meeting the Standards Unit 1*, p. 60

During Reading

Teach the Selection(s)

Choose from the following resources to teach the selection(s):

_____ During Reading, *SE/ATE*, pp. 64–70

_____ History Connection: Civil Rights, *ATE*, p. 69

_____ Reading Skills: Skim and Scan, *ATE*, p. 66

_____ Vocabulary Skills: Idioms, *ATE*, p. 67

_____ Grammar Skills: Punctuate Dialogue, *ATE*, p. 69

_____ Build Vocabulary, *Meeting the Standards Unit 1*, p. 61

_____ Analyze Literature: Allusion, *Meeting the Standards Unit 1*, p. 62

Differentiate Instruction

Consider the following alternative teaching options to differentiate instruction:

_____ Enrichment, *ATE*, p. 65

_____ Reading Proficiency, *ATE*, p. 68

_____ Kinesthetic Learning, *ATE*, p. 68

_____ Visual Learning, *ATE*, p. 70

_____ English Language Learning, *ATE*, p. 70

_____ Analyze Cause and Effect, *Differentiated Instruction for Advanced Students*, pp. 5–6

_____ Reading Strategies and Skills Practice: Make Connections, *Differentiated Instruction for Developing Readers*, p. 4

_____ Analyze Cause and Effect, *Differentiated Instruction for English Language Learners*, p. 19

After Reading

Review and Extend
Use the following materials to review and extend the lesson:
____ After Reading, *SE/ATE*, p. 71
____ Analyze Literature: Characterization, *Meeting the Standards Unit 1*, p. 64

Teach the Workshop(s)
Select from the following materials to teach the workshop(s):
____ Grammar & Style: Nominative and Objective Pronouns, *SE/ATE*, p. 72
____ Language Arts Handbook Section 3.4, Pronouns, *SE/ATE*, pp. 856–858
____ Subject and Object Pronouns, *Exceeding the Standards: Grammar & Style*, pp. 40–42

Assess
Administer the following assessment tool(s):
____ Selection Quiz, *Meeting the Standards Unit 1*, p. 65
____ Lesson Test, *Assessment Guide*, p. 37

Technology Tools
Enhance the lesson with interactive activities offered in these technology supplements:

- EMC Launchpad
- Annotated Teacher's Edition on CD
- Interactive Student Text on CD
- Exam*View*® Assessment Suite on CD
- Visual Teaching Package
- ETS Online Criterion-Based Essay Grader (Grades 9–12)
- EMC Audio Library
- EMC E-Library
- **mirrorsandwindows.com**

Name: _____ Date: _____

M   T   W   Th   F

The Foghorn / The Aqualung, p. 73

Directed Reading
- **Reading Level:** Moderate
- **Difficulty Consideration:** Vocabulary
- **Ease Factor:** Style

Pacing
- **Regular Schedule:** 3 days
- **Block Schedule:** 1.5 days

Objectives
Studying this lesson will enable students to
- use reading skills such as context clues
- analyze mood
- experience Ray Bradbury's style of storytelling
- synthesize content from different texts

Before Reading

Preview and Motivate
Choose from the following materials to preview the lesson and motivate your students:
_____ Before Reading, *SE/ATE*, p. 73
_____ Build Background: Connect to Personal Experience, *Meeting the Standards Unit 1*, p. 67
_____ Build Vocabulary: Parts of Speech, *Meeting the Standards Unit 1*, p. 68

During Reading

Teach the Selection(s)
Choose from the following resources to teach the selection(s):
_____ During Reading, *SE/ATE*, pp. 74–82
_____ Science Connection: Sea Creatures, *ATE*, p. 79
_____ Informational Text Connection: "The Aqualung," *ATE*, p. 83
_____ Vocabulary Skills: Concrete and Abstract Nouns, *ATE*, p. 77
_____ Research Skills: Multimedia Sources, *ATE*, p. 79
_____ Speaking & Listening Skills: Discuss Literary Elements, *ATE*, p. 81
_____ Reading Skills: Compare and Contrast, *ATE*, p. 82
_____ Analyze Literature: Personification, *Meeting the Standards Unit 1*, p. 70

Differentiate Instruction
Consider the following alternative teaching options to differentiate instruction:
_____ English Language Learning, *ATE*, p. 75
_____ Reading Proficiency, *ATE*, pp. 76, 80
_____ Enrichment, *ATE*, pp. 76, 78
_____ Visual Learning, *ATE*, p. 80
_____ Reading Strategies and Skills Practice: Visualize, *Differentiated Instruction for Developing Readers*, p. 7
_____ Reading Strategies and Skills Practice: Use Text Organization, *Differentiated Instruction for Developing Readers*, p. 10

After Reading

Review and Extend

Use the following materials to review and extend the lesson:

_____ After Reading, *SE/ATE*, pp. 82, 84

_____ Use Reading Strategies: Make Connections, *Meeting the Standards Unit 1*, p. 71

Assess

Administer the following assessment tool(s):

_____ Selection Quiz, *Meeting the Standards Unit 1*, p. 72

_____ Lesson Test, *Assessment Guide*, p. 40

Technology Tools

Enhance the lesson with interactive activities offered in these technology supplements:

- EMC Launchpad
- Annotated Teacher's Edition on CD
- Interactive Student Text on CD
- Exam*View*® Assessment Suite on CD
- Visual Teaching Package
- ETS Online Criterion-Based Essay Grader (Grades 9–12)
- EMC Audio Library
- EMC E-Library
- **mirrorsandwindows.com**

Name: _____ Date: _____
M   T   W   Th   F

Rikki-Tikki-Tavi / The Green Mamba, p. 85

Directed Reading
"Rikki-Tikki-Tavi"
- **Reading Level:** Moderate
- **Difficulty Consideration:** Many characters, selection length
- **Ease Factor:** Vocabulary

"The Green Mamba"
- **Reading Level:** Moderate
- **Difficulty Consideration:** Unfamiliar setting, long sentences
- **Ease Factor:** Exciting events

Pacing
- **Regular Schedule:** 4 days
- **Block Schedule:** 2 days

Objectives
Studying this lesson will enable students to
- compare literary selections of different genres
- use reading skills such as previewing texts
- describe personification
- name literary accomplishments of Rudyard Kipling and Roald Dahl
- observe skills that help people and animals handle the unexpected

Before Reading

Preview and Motivate
Choose from the following materials to preview the lesson and motivate your students:
_____   Before Reading, *SE/ATE*, p. 85
_____   Build Background, *Meeting the Standards Unit 1*, p. 73
_____   Set Purpose, *Meeting the Standards Unit 1*, p. 73
_____   Practice Vocabulary, *Meeting the Standards Unit 1*, p. 73

During Reading

Teach the Selection(s)
Choose from the following resources to teach the selection(s):
_____   During Reading, *SE/ATE*, pp. 86–103
_____   Writing Skills: Figurative Language, *ATE*, p. 89
_____   Grammar Skills: Semicolons and Dashes, *ATE*, p. 91
_____   Reading Skills: Identify Multiple Levels of Meaning, *ATE*, p. 93
_____   Reading Skills: Summarize, *ATE*, p. 95
_____   Vocabulary Skills: Foreign Words in English, *ATE*, p. 96
_____   Writing Skills: Develop a Personified Character, *ATE*, p. 97
_____   Writing Skills: Use Similes, *ATE*, p. 99
_____   Grammar Skills: Ellipses, *ATE*, p. 101
_____   Speaking & Listening Skills: Prepare an Informal Debate, *ATE*, p. 103
_____   Compare Literature: Personification, *Meeting the Standards Unit 1*, p. 74

Differentiate Instruction

Consider the following alternative teaching options to differentiate instruction:

_____ Reading Proficiency, *ATE*, pp. 87, 98

_____ Visual Learning, *ATE*, p. 87

_____ English Language Learning, *ATE*, pp. 88, 92, 94, 100, 102

_____ Auditory Learning, *ATE*, pp. 88, 94

_____ Kinesthetic Learning, *ATE*, p. 90

_____ Enrichment, *ATE*, p. 92

_____ Understand Literary Elements: Personification, *Differentiated Instruction for English Language Learners*, p. 32

_____ Understand Literary Elements: Plot, *Differentiated Instruction for English Language Learners*, p. 51

After Reading

Review and Extend

Use the following materials to review and extend the lesson:

_____ After Reading, *SE/ATE*, pp. 97, 104

_____ Compare Literature: Personification (continued), *Meeting the Standards Unit 1*, p. 75

_____ Compare Literature: Character Traits, *Meeting the Standards Unit 1*, p. 76

_____ Make Connections, *Meeting the Standards Unit 1*, p. 77

_____ What Do You Think? *Meeting the Standards Unit 1*, p. 80

_____ Identifying Parts of Speech, *Exceeding the Standards: Grammar & Style 1*, pp. 16–19

Assess

Administer the following assessment tool(s):

_____ Selection Quiz: Focus on "Rikki-Tikki-Tavi," *Meeting the Standards Unit 1*, p. 78

_____ Selection Quiz: Focus on "The Green Mamba," *Meeting the Standards Unit 1*, p. 79

_____ Lesson Test, *Assessment Guide*, p. 43

Technology Tools

Enhance the lesson with interactive activities offered in these technology supplements:

- EMC Launchpad
- Annotated Teacher's Edition on CD
- Interactive Student Text on CD
- Exam*View*® Assessment Suite on CD
- Visual Teaching Package
- ETS Online Criterion-Based Essay Grader (Grades 9–12)
- EMC Audio Library
- EMC E-Library
- **mirrorsandwindows.com**

Name: _____ Date: _____

Uncle Tony's Goat, p. 105

Independent Reading
- **Reading Level:** Easy
- **Difficulty Consideration:** None
- **Ease Factor:** Simple plot

Pacing
- **Regular Schedule:** 1 day
- **Block Schedule:** 0.5 day

Objectives
Studying this lesson will enable students to
- read with developing fluency
- read silently with comprehension for a sustained period of time

Before Reading

Preview and Motivate
Choose from the following materials to preview the lesson and motivate your students:
_____ Before Reading, *SE/ATE*, p. 105
_____ Vocabulary, *Meeting the Standards Unit 1*, p. 81
_____ Set Purpose, *Meeting the Standards Unit 1*, p. 82

During Reading

Teach the Selection(s)
Choose from the following resources to teach the selection(s):
_____ During Reading, *SE/ATE*, pp. 105–110
_____ Grammar Skills: Progressive Verb Forms, *ATE*, p. 108
_____ Reading Skills: Use Graphic Organizers, *ATE*, p. 109
_____ Questions to Answer as You Read, *Meeting the Standards Unit 1*, p. 83

Differentiate Instruction
Consider the following alternative teaching options to differentiate instruction:
_____ English Language Learning, *ATE*, p. 107
_____ Enrichment, *ATE*, p. 110
_____ Visual Learning, *ATE*, p. 110
_____ Independent Reading Project: Native American Literature, *Differentiated Instruction for Advanced Students*, pp. 7–8

After Reading

Review and Extend
Use the following materials to review and extend the lesson:
_____ After Reading, *SE/ATE*, p. 110
_____ Describe and Critique: Fiction, *Meeting the Standards Unit 1*, p. 86

Assess

Administer the following assessment tool(s):

_____ Selection Quiz, *Meeting the Standards Unit 1,* p. 84

_____ Lesson Test, *Assessment Guide,* p. 46

Technology Tools

Enhance the lesson with interactive activities offered in these technology supplements:

- EMC Launchpad
- Annotated Teacher's Edition on CD
- Interactive Student Text on CD
- Exam*View*® Assessment Suite on CD
- Visual Teaching Package
- ETS Online Criterion-Based Essay Grader (Grades 9–12)
- EMC Audio Library
- EMC E-Library
- **mirrorsandwindows.com**

Name: _____   Date: _____
                                                          M   T   W   Th   F

The Serial Garden, p. 111

Independent Reading
- **Reading Level:** Challenging
- **Difficulty Consideration:** Length and vocabulary
- **Ease Factor:** Opening lines

Pacing
- **Regular Schedule:** 2 days
- **Block Schedule:** 1 day

Objectives
Studying this lesson will enable students to
- read with developing fluency
- read silently with comprehension for a sustained period of time

---

Before Reading

Preview and Motivate
Choose from the following materials to preview the lesson and motivate your students:
_____   Before Reading, *SE/ATE*, p. 111
_____   Vocabulary, *Meeting the Standards Unit 1*, p. 88

During Reading

Teach the Selection(s)
Choose from the following resources to teach the selection(s):
_____   During Reading, *SE/ATE*, pp. 111–124
_____   Reading Skills: Take Notes, *ATE*, p. 114
_____   Writing Skills: Precise Language, *ATE*, p. 115
_____   Vocabulary Skills: Words from Mythology, *ATE*, p. 117
_____   Vocabulary Skills: Context Clues: Appositives, *ATE*, p. 119
_____   Grammar Skills: Verbs with Indefinite Pronouns, *ATE*, p. 121
_____   Grammar Skills: Commonly Confused Words, *ATE*, p. 122
_____   Grammar Skills: Commas in a Series, *ATE*, p. 123
_____   Complete a Story Events Chart, *Meeting the Standards Unit 1*, p. 89
_____   Analyze Literature, *Meeting the Standards Unit 1*, p. 90

Differentiate Instruction
Consider the following alternative teaching options to differentiate instruction:
_____   Reading Proficiency, *ATE*, p. 113
_____   Enrichment, *ATE*, pp. 113, 124
_____   English Language Learning, *ATE*, p. 116
_____   Kinesthetic Learning, *ATE*, p. 118
_____   Auditory and Kinesthetic Learning, *ATE*, p. 120

After Reading

Review and Extend
Use the following materials to review and extend the lesson:
_____   After Reading, *SE/ATE*, p. 124
_____   Write a New Ending, *Meeting the Standards Unit 1*, p. 91
_____   Describe and Critique: Fiction, *Meeting the Standards Unit 1*, p. 92

Assess

Administer the following assessment tool(s):

_____ Lesson Test, *Assessment Guide*, p. 49

Technology Tools

Enhance the lesson with interactive activities offered in these technology supplements:

- EMC Launchpad
- Annotated Teacher's Edition on CD
- Interactive Student Text on CD
- Exam*View*® Assessment Suite on CD
- Visual Teaching Package
- ETS Online Criterion-Based Essay Grader (Grades 9–12)
- EMC Audio Library
- EMC E-Library
- **mirrorsandwindows.com**

Name: _____

Date: _____
M   T   W   Th   F

Writing Workshop: Expository Writing—Responding to a Short Story, p. 126

Pacing
- **Regular Schedule:** 3 days
- **Block Schedule:** 1.5 days

Objectives
Participating in this lesson will help enable students to
- write a literary response essay that has an effective introduction
- write a literary response essay that has a clear thesis statement
- write a literary response essay that has a clear organizational pattern
- write a literary response essay that has a conclusion restating the thesis

---

Teach the Workshop
Select from the following resources to teach the workshop:
_____ Expository Writing: Responding to a Short Story, *SE/ATE*, pp. 126–131
_____ Writing Skills: Topic Sentences, *ATE*, p. 129
_____ Writing Skills: Outlines, *ATE*, p. 131
_____ Language Arts Handbook Section 4.1, The Writing Process, *SE/ATE*, pp. 888–897

Differentiate Instruction
Consider the following alternative teaching options to differentiate instruction:
_____ Reading Proficiency, *ATE*, pp. 127, 130
_____ English Language Learning, *ATE*, pp. 127, 128
_____ Enrichment, *ATE*, p. 128

Review and Extend
Use the following materials to review and extend the lesson:
_____ Narrative Writing: Tell About a Person in Action, *Exceeding the Standards: Writing*, pp. 1–6

Technology Tools
Enhance the lesson with interactive activities offered in these technology supplements:
- EMC Launchpad
- Annotated Teacher's Edition on CD
- Interactive Student Text on CD
- Exam*View*® Assessment Suite on CD
- Visual Teaching Package
- ETS Online Criterion-Based Essay Grader (Grades 9–12)
- EMC Audio Library
- EMC E-Library
- **mirrorsandwindows.com**

Name: _____ Date: _____

Speaking & Listening Workshop: Giving and Actively Listening to Oral Summaries, p. 132

Pacing
- **Regular Schedule:** 2 days
- **Block Schedule:** 1 day

Objectives
Participating in this lesson will help enable students to
- deliver an oral summary of a short story that clearly presents the main details of the plot
- deliver an oral summary of a short story that conveys the setting and characters using sensory details

Teach the Workshop
Select from the following resources to teach the workshop:

____ Speaking & Listening: Giving and Actively Listening to Oral Summaries, *SE/ATE*, pp. 132–133

____ Speaking & Listening Skills: Using Inflection, *ATE*, p. 133

____ Language Arts Handbook Section 7.1, Verbal and Nonverbal Communication, *SE/ATE*, p. 912

____ Language Arts Handbook Section 7.2, Listening Skills, *SE/ATE*, pp. 913–914

____ Language Arts Handbook Section 7.6, Public Speaking, *SE/ATE*, pp. 916–917

Differentiate Instruction
Consider the following alternative teaching options to differentiate instruction:

____ English Language Learning, *ATE*, p. 132

Review and Extend
Use the following materials to review and extend the lesson:

____ Read Fiction Aloud, *Exceeding the Standards: Literature & Reading*, pp. 3–5

____ Giving and Actively Listening to Oral Summaries, *Exceeding the Standards: Speaking & Listening*, pp. 1–3

Technology Tools
Enhance the lesson with interactive activities offered in these technology supplements:

- EMC Launchpad
- Annotated Teacher's Edition on CD
- Interactive Student Text on CD
- Exam*View*® Assessment Suite on CD
- Visual Teaching Package
- ETS Online Criterion-Based Essay Grader (Grades 9–12)
- EMC Audio Library
- EMC E-Library
- **mirrorsandwindows.com**

LESSON PLAN

Test Practice Workshop, p. 134

Pacing
- **Regular Schedule:** 1 day
- **Block Schedule:** 0.5 day

Objectives
Participating in this lesson will help enable students to
- write a response to literature based on a timed writing prompt

- answer standardized test questions that demonstrate revising and editing skills
- demonstrate the ability to make inferences from a reading by answering standardized questions

---

Teach the Workshop
Select from the following resources to teach the workshop:
_____ Writing Skills: Literary Response, *SE/ATE*, p. 134
_____ Revising and Editing Skills, *SE/ATE*, p. 135
_____ Reading Skills, *SE/ATE*, pp. 136–137
_____ Rubric for a Response to Literature, *ATE*, p. 134
_____ Test-Taking Skills: Eliminate Incorrect Responses, *ATE*, p. 137
_____ Language Arts Handbook Section 8.4, Answering Multiple-Choice Questions, *SE/ATE*, p. 923
_____ Language Arts Handbook Section 8.5, Answering Reading Comprehension Questions, *SE/ATE*, p. 923
_____ Test-Taking Strategies and Skills, *Exceeding the Standards: Test Practice*, pp. 1–4

Differentiate Instruction
Consider the following alternative teaching options to differentiate instruction:
_____ English Language Learning, *ATE*, p. 136

Review and Extend
Use the following materials to review and extend the lesson:
_____ Fiction Study Guide: Practice Test, *Meeting the Standards Unit 1*, pp. 11–17
_____ Literary Response Practice Test: Reading, *Exceeding the Standards: Test Practice*, pp. 5–6

Technology Tools
Enhance the lesson with interactive activities offered in these technology supplements:
- EMC Launchpad
- Annotated Teacher's Edition on CD
- Interactive Student Text on CD
- Exam*View*® Assessment Suite on CD
- Visual Teaching Package
- ETS Online Criterion-Based Essay Grader (Grades 9–12)
- EMC Audio Library
- EMC E-Library
- **mirrorsandwindows.com**

Name: _____   Date: _____

M   T   W   Th   F

Unit 2 Fiction Opener, p. 138

Pacing	Objectives
• **Regular Schedule:** 1 day • **Block Schedule:** 0.5 day	Studying this lesson will enable students to • connect the themes expressed in a selection to their own lives

Plan the Unit
Use the following resources to plan instruction for this unit:

_____ Unit 2 Visual Planning Guide: Unit-Based Resources, *ATE*, pp. 138A–138B

_____ Unit 2 Visual Planning Guide: Lesson-by-Lesson Resources, *ATE*, pp. 138C–138D

_____ Unit 2 Scope & Sequence Guide, *ATE*, pp. 138E–138H

_____ Unit 2 Building Vocabulary, *ATE*, pp. 138I–138J

_____ Launch the Unit, *ATE*, p. 138

Teach the Unit Opener
Choose from the following resources to teach the unit opener:

_____ Unit 2 Overview, *SE/ATE*, pp. 138–139

_____ Fiction Study Guide: Introduction, *Meeting the Standards Unit 2*, p. 1

_____ Fiction Study Guide: Reviewing Plot and Applying Plot to the Selections, *Meeting the Standards Unit 2*, pp. 6–7

_____ Fiction Study Guide: Reviewing Characters and Applying Characters to the Selections, *Meeting the Standards Unit 2*, pp. 8–9

_____ Fiction Study Guide: Reviewing Setting and Applying Setting to the Selections, *Meeting the Standards Unit 2*, p. 10

_____ Fiction Study Guide: Master Vocabulary List, *Meeting the Standards Unit 2*, p. 18

Extend the Unit
Choose from the following resources to extend the unit:

_____ For Your Reading List, *SE/ATE*, p. 237

_____ Unit 2, *Exceeding the Standards: Grammar & Style*, pp. 20–48

_____ Lifelong Learning: The Definition of Character: Part 2, *Exceeding the Standards: Special Topics*, pp. 6–7

_____ Media Literacy: Using Microsoft Word, *Exceeding the Standards: Special Topics*, pp. 8–9

_____ Unit 2, *Exceeding the Standards: Vocabulary & Spelling*, pp. 13–20

Assess
Administer the following assessment tool(s):

_____ Formative Surveys 1 and 2, *Assessment Guide*, pp. 3–20

_____ Reading Fluency Assessments, Passages 1 and 2, *Assessment Guide*, pp. 295–296

_____ Unit 2 Exam, *Assessment Guide*, pp. 257–260

Technology Tools

Enhance the lesson with interactive activities offered in these technology supplements:

- EMC Launchpad
- Annotated Teacher's Edition on CD
- Interactive Student Text on CD
- Exam*View*® Assessment Suite on CD
- Visual Teaching Package
- ETS Online Criterion-Based Essay Grader (Grades 9–12)
- EMC Audio Library
- EMC E-Library
- **mirrorsandwindows.com**

Name: _____ Date: _____

M   T   W   Th   F

Literary Element: Understanding Point of View, p. 140

Hollywood and the Pits, p. 141

Guided Reading: Reading Model	**Objectives**
• **Reading Level:** Moderate	Studying this lesson will enable students to
• **Difficulty Consideration:** Two narrative voices	• use reading skills such as analyzing cause and effect
• **Ease Factor:** Familiar themes	• define point of view and recognize its effect in the selection
Pacing	• describe how Cherylene Lee establishes mood and tone
• **Regular Schedule:** 3 days	• appreciate a story based on the author's personal experiences
• **Block Schedule:** 1.5 days	

Before Reading

Teach the Feature(s)

Select from the following resources to teach the feature(s):

_____ Literary Element: Understanding Point of View, *SE/ATE*, p. 140

_____ Differentiated Instruction: Enrichment, *ATE*, p. 140

_____ Differentiated Instruction: Visual Learning, *ATE*, p. 140

_____ Fiction Study Guide: Understanding Point of View and Applying Point of View to the Selections, *Meeting the Standards Unit 2*, pp. 2–3

Preview and Motivate

Choose from the following materials to preview the lesson and motivate your students:

_____ Fiction Reading Model, *SE/ATE*, p. 8

_____ Before Reading, *SE/ATE*, p. 141

_____ Build Vocabulary, *Meeting the Standards Unit 2*, p. 19

_____ Journal Response, *Meeting the Standards Unit 2*, p. 20

During Reading

Teach the Selection(s)

Choose from the following resources to teach the selection(s):

_____ During Reading, *SE/ATE*, pp. 142–151

_____ Science Connection: Geologic Time, *ATE*, p. 148

_____ Reading Skills: Monitor Comprehension, *ATE*, p. 145

_____ Grammar Skills: Passive Voice and Active Voice, *ATE*, p. 147

_____ Vocabulary Skills: Jargon, *ATE*, p. 148

_____ Research Skills: Primary and Secondary Sources, *ATE*, p. 149

_____ Writing Skills: Cause-and-Effect Order, *ATE*, p. 151

_____ Analyze Literature: Character, *Meeting the Standards Unit 2*, p. 21

Differentiate Instruction

Consider the following alternative teaching options to differentiate instruction:

_____ Reading Proficiency, *ATE*, p. 143
_____ Auditory Learning, *ATE*, p. 143
_____ English Language Learning, *ATE*, pp. 144, 146
_____ Visual Learning, *ATE*, p. 146
_____ Enrichment, *ATE*, p. 150
_____ Reading Strategies and Skills Practice: Take Notes, *Differentiated Instruction for Developing Readers*, pp. 13–15

After Reading

Review and Extend

Use the following materials to review and extend the lesson:

_____ After Reading, *SE/ATE*, p. 152
_____ Use Reading Skills: Cause and Effect, *Meeting the Standards Unit 2*, p. 22
_____ Extend Understanding: Creative Writing, *Meeting the Standards Unit 2*, p. 23
_____ Media Literacy: Dig for Details, *Exceeding the Standards: Extension Activities*, pp. 5–6
_____ Subject and Object Pronouns, *Exceeding the Standards: Grammar & Style*, pp. 40–42

Assess

Administer the following assessment tool(s):

_____ Selection Quiz, *Meeting the Standards Unit 2*, p. 24
_____ Lesson Test, *Assessment Guide*, pp. 52–54

Technology Tools

Enhance the lesson with interactive activities offered in these technology supplements:

- EMC Launchpad
- Annotated Teacher's Edition on CD
- Interactive Student Text on CD
- Exam*View*® Assessment Suite on CD
- Visual Teaching Package
- ETS Online Criterion-Based Essay Grader (Grades 9–12)
- EMC Audio Library
- EMC E-Library
- **mirrorsandwindows.com**

Name: _____ Date: _____

M   T   W   Th   F

Literary Element: Understanding Theme, p. 153

The Scholarship Jacket, p. 155

Grammar & Style Workshop: Comma Use, p. 162

Guided Reading: Reading Model
- **Reading Level:** Easy
- **Difficulty Consideration:** None
- **Ease Factor:** Familiar themes

Pacing
- **Regular Schedule:** 3 days
- **Block Schedule:** 1.5 days

Objectives
Studying this lesson will enable students to
- use reading skills such as context clues
- identify a theme by examining characterization, dialogue, and plot
- infer Marta Salinas's purpose and explore how she achieves it
- appreciate a story about justice

Before Reading

Teach the Feature(s)
Select from the following resources to teach the feature(s):
_____   Literary Element: Understanding Theme, *SE/ATE*, p. 153
_____   Writing Skills: Explore Themes Through Freewriting, *SE/ATE*, p. 153
_____   Fiction Study Guide: Understanding Theme and Applying Theme, *Meeting the Standards Unit 2*, pp. 4–5

Preview and Motivate
Choose from the following materials to preview the lesson and motivate your students:
_____   Fiction Reading Model, *SE/ATE*, p. 8
_____   Before Reading, *SE/ATE*, p. 154
_____   Build Background, *Meeting the Standards Unit 2*, p. 25
_____   Set Purpose, *Meeting the Standards Unit 2*, p. 26
_____   Practice Vocabulary, *Meeting the Standards Unit 2*, p. 27

During Reading

Teach the Selection(s)
Choose from the following resources to teach the selection(s):
_____   During Reading, *SE/ATE*, pp. 155–160
_____   Reading Skills: Identify Author's Purpose, *ATE*, p. 157
_____   Grammar Skills: Subordinating Conjunctions, *ATE*, p. 158
_____   Speaking & Listening Skills: Persuasive Speech, *ATE*, p. 159
_____   Analyze Literature: Plot, *Meeting the Standards Unit 2*, p. 28

Differentiate Instruction

Consider the following alternative teaching options to differentiate instruction:

____ Reading Proficiency, *ATE*, p. 156

____ English Language Learning, *ATE*, p. 156

____ Enrichment, *ATE*, p. 160

____ Theme Study: Multiple Themes and Levels of Meaning, *Differentiated Instruction for Advanced Students*, p. 9

After Reading

Review and Extend

Use the following materials to review and extend the lesson:

____ After Reading, *SE/ATE*, p. 161

____ Analyze Literature: Theme, *Meeting the Standards Unit 2*, p. 29

Teach the Workshop(s)

Select from the following materials to teach the workshop(s):

____ Grammar & Style: Comma Use, *SE/ATE*, p. 162

____ Language Arts Handbook Section 3.15, Punctuation, *SE/ATE*, pp. 876–881

____ Commas, *Exceeding the Standards: Grammar & Style*, pp. 159–162

Assess

Administer the following assessment tool(s):

____ Selection Quiz, *Meeting the Standards Unit 2,* pp. 30–31

____ Lesson Test, *Assessment Guide*, pp. 55–57

Technology Tools

Enhance the lesson with interactive activities offered in these technology supplements:

- EMC Launchpad
- Annotated Teacher's Edition on CD
- Interactive Student Text on CD
- Exam*View*® Assessment Suite on CD
- Visual Teaching Package
- ETS Online Criterion-Based Essay Grader (Grades 9–12)
- EMC Audio Library
- EMC E-Library
- **mirrorsandwindows.com**

Name: _____ Date: _____

M   T   W   Th   F

Amigo Brothers / *from* The Greatest: Muhammad Ali, p. 163

Vocabulary & Spelling Workshop: Prefixes, Roots, and Suffixes, p. 176

Directed Reading
- **Reading Level:** Moderate
- **Difficulty Consideration:** Vocabulary
- **Ease Factor:** Vivid description

Pacing
- **Regular Schedule:** 3 days
- **Block Schedule:** 1.5 days

Objectives

Studying this lesson will enable students to
- use reading skills such as drawing conclusions
- define point of view and recognize the effect of a third-person omniscient narrator in the selection
- describe the work of Piri Thomas and see how his personal experiences influenced his writing
- appreciate a story about the endurance of true friendship

Before Reading

Preview and Motivate

Choose from the following materials to preview the lesson and motivate your students:

_____ Before Reading, *SE/ATE*, p. 163

_____ Practice Vocabulary, *Meeting the Standards Unit 2*, p. 32

During Reading

Teach the Selection(s)

Choose from the following resources to teach the selection(s):

_____ During Reading, *SE/ATE*, pp. 164–172

_____ Informational Text Connection: from *The Greatest: Muhammad Ali*, *SE/ATE*, pp. 173–174

_____ Grammar Skills: Adverb Clause, *ATE*, p. 167

_____ Vocabulary Skills: Idioms, *ATE*, p. 168

_____ Reading Skills: Identify Author's Purpose, *ATE*, p. 169

_____ Speaking & Listening Skills: Dramatic Reading, *ATE*, p. 171

_____ Analyze Literature: Character, *Meeting the Standards Unit 2*, p. 33

_____ Analyze Literature: Point of View, *Meeting the Standards Unit 2*, p. 34

_____ Point of View and Author's Purpose, *Meeting the Standards Unit 2*, p. 37

Differentiate Instruction

Consider the following alternative teaching options to differentiate instruction:

_____ English Language Learning, *ATE*, pp. 165, 166

_____ Reading Proficiency, *ATE*, pp. 165, 166

_____ Visual Learning, *ATE*, p. 170

_____ Enrichment, *ATE*, p. 172

_____ Author Study: Piri Thomas, *Differentiated Instruction for Advanced Students*, pp. 10–11

After Reading

Review and Extend
Use the following materials to review and extend the lesson:

____ After Reading, *SE/ATE*, pp. 172, 175

____ Vocabulary & Spelling: Prefixes, Roots, and Suffixes, *SE/ATE*, p. 176

____ Analyze Literature: Pros and Cons, *Meeting the Standards Unit 2*, p. 35

____ Analyze Literature: Fiction, *Meeting the Standards Unit 2*, p. 36

____ Common and Proper Nouns, *Exceeding the Standards: Grammar & Style*, pp. 20–22

Teach the Workshop(s)
Select from the following materials to teach the workshop(s):

____ Vocabulary & Spelling: Prefixes, Roots, and Suffixes, *SE/ATE*, p. 176

____ Language Arts Handbook Section 2.2, Breaking Words into Base Words, Word Roots, Prefixes, and Suffixes, *SE/ATE*, pp. 837–840

____ Word Roots, Prefixes, and Suffixes, *Exceeding the Standards: Vocabulary & Spelling*, pp. 47–48

____ Prefixes and Similar Word Parts, *Exceeding the Standards: Vocabulary & Spelling*, pp. 49–50

____ Suffixes, *Exceeding the Standards: Vocabulary & Spelling*, pp. 51–52

Assess
Administer the following assessment tool(s):

____ Selection Quiz, *Meeting the Standards Unit 2,* pp. 41–42

____ Lesson Test, *Assessment Guide*, pp. 58–60

Technology Tools
Enhance the lesson with interactive activities offered in these technology supplements:

- EMC Launchpad
- Annotated Teacher's Edition on CD
- Interactive Student Text on CD
- Exam*View*® Assessment Suite on CD
- Visual Teaching Package
- ETS Online Criterion-Based Essay Grader (Grades 9–12)
- EMC Audio Library
- EMC E-Library
- **mirrorsandwindows.com**

Name: _____ Date: _____

M T W Th F

Four Skinny Trees, p. 177

Directed Reading
- **Reading Level:** Easy
- **Difficulty Consideration:** Imagery
- **Ease Factor:** Length

Pacing
- **Regular Schedule:** 1 day
- **Block Schedule:** 0.5 day

Objectives
Studying this lesson will enable students to
- use reading strategies such as asking questions

- define description and recognize the literal and figurative meanings of sensory language
- describe the literary accomplishments of Sandra Cisneros, recognize how her Mexican heritage and childhood experiences inspired her work, and appreciate how she applies poetic techniques to prose
- read a story on the themes of alienation, identity, and struggle

Before Reading

Preview and Motivate
Choose from the following materials to preview the lesson and motivate your students:
_____ Before Reading, *SE/ATE*, p. 177
_____ Set Purpose, *Meeting the Standards Unit 2*, p. 43

During Reading

Teach the Selection(s)
Choose from the following resources to teach the selection(s):
_____ During Reading, *SE/ATE*, pp. 178–179
_____ Analyze Literature: Description, *Meeting the Standards Unit 2*, p. 44

Differentiate Instruction
Consider the following alternative teaching options to differentiate instruction:
_____ Reading Proficiency, *ATE*, p. 179

After Reading

Review and Extend
Use the following materials to review and extend the lesson:
_____ After Reading, *SE/ATE*, p. 180
_____ Analyze Literature: Fiction, *Meeting the Standards Unit 2*, p. 45

Assess
Administer the following assessment tool(s):
_____ Selection Quiz, *Meeting the Standards Unit 2*, p. 46
_____ Lesson Test, *Assessment Guide*, pp. 61–63

Technology Tools

Enhance the lesson with interactive activities offered in these technology supplements:

- EMC Launchpad
- Annotated Teacher's Edition on CD
- Interactive Student Text on CD
- Exam*View*® Assessment Suite on CD
- Visual Teaching Package
- ETS Online Criterion-Based Essay Grader (Grades 9–12)
- EMC Audio Library
- EMC E-Library
- **mirrorsandwindows.com**

Name: _____ Date: _____

M   T   W   Th   F

The White Umbrella, p. 181

Grammar & Style Workshop: Independent and Dependent Clauses, p. 190

Directed Reading
- **Reading Level:** Easy
- **Difficulty Consideration:** None
- **Ease Factor:** Familiar themes

Pacing
- **Regular Schedule:** 2 days
- **Block Schedule:** 1 day

Objectives

Studying this lesson will enable students to
- use reading skills such as comparing and contrasting
- define mood and recognize how descriptive language and sensory details contribute to the mood
- describe the literary accomplishments of Gish Jen and how her Chinese-American heritage influences her writing
- appreciate a story about the desire to belong and family loyalty

---

Before Reading

Preview and Motivate

Choose from the following materials to preview the lesson and motivate your students:

_____   Before Reading, *SE/ATE*, p. 181
_____   Vocabulary, *Meeting the Standards Unit 2*, p. 47
_____   Journal Response, *Meeting the Standards Unit 2*, p. 48

During Reading

Teach the Selection(s)

Choose from the following resources to teach the selection(s):

_____   During Reading, *SE/ATE*, pp. 182–188
_____   Reading Skills: Ask Questions, *ATE*, p. 184
_____   Writing Skills: Sensory Details, *ATE*, p. 186
_____   Analyze Literature: Mood, *Meeting the Standards Unit 2*, p. 49

Differentiate Instruction

Consider the following alternative teaching options to differentiate instruction:

_____   Reading Proficiency, *ATE*, pp. 183, 185
_____   Visual Learning, *ATE*, p. 183
_____   Enrichment, *ATE*, p. 187
_____   Kinesthetic Learning, *ATE*, p. 188

After Reading

Review and Extend

Use the following materials to review and extend the lesson:

_____   After Reading, *SE/ATE*, p. 189
_____   Use Reading Skills: Cause and Effect, *Meeting the Standards Unit 2*, p. 50
_____   Analyze Literature: Fiction, *Meeting the Standards Unit 2*, p. 51

Teach the Workshop(s)

Select from the following materials to teach the workshop(s):

____ Grammar & Style: Independent and Dependent Clauses, *SE/ATE*, p. 190

____ Language Arts Handbook Section 3.12, Clauses, *SE/ATE*, p. 868

____ Types of Clauses with a Sentence, *Exceeding the Standards: Grammar & Style*, pp. 144–150

____ The Clauses of a Sentence: Simple and Compound Sentences, *Exceeding the Standards: Grammar & Style*, pp. 151–152

____ The Clauses of a Sentence: Complex Sentences, *Exceeding the Standards: Grammar & Style*, pp. 153–155

Assess

Administer the following assessment tool(s):

____ Selection Quiz, *Meeting the Standards Unit 2*, pp. 52–53

____ Lesson Test, *Assessment Guide*, pp. 64–66

Technology Tools

Enhance the lesson with interactive activities offered in these technology supplements:

- EMC Launchpad
- Annotated Teacher's Edition on CD
- Interactive Student Text on CD
- Exam*View*® Assessment Suite on CD
- Visual Teaching Package
- ETS Online Criterion-Based Essay Grader (Grades 9–12)
- EMC Audio Library
- EMC E-Library
- **mirrorsandwindows.com**

LESSON PLAN

Name: _____ Date: _____

Jed's Grandfather / The Courage That My Mother Had, p. 191

Directed Reading
"Jed's Grandfather"
- **Reading Level:** Moderate
- **Difficulty Consideration:** Subject matter
- **Ease Factor:** Length

"The Courage That My Mother Had"
- **Reading Level:** Easy
- **Difficulty Consideration:** Metaphors
- **Ease Factor:** Length

Pacing
- **Regular Schedule:** 3 days
- **Block Schedule:** 1.5 days

Objectives
Studying this lesson will enable students to
- compare literary selections of different genres
- use reading strategies such as asking questions and clarifying
- define tone and recognize how a writer establishes tone
- compare the effects of tone in two literary works
- enjoy literature about the wisdom strength of elders

Before Reading

Preview and Motivate
Choose from the following materials to preview the lesson and motivate your students:
_____   Before Reading, *SE/ATE*, p. 191
_____   Build Background, Set Purpose, and Practice Vocabulary, *Meeting the Standards Unit 2*, p. 54

During Reading

Teach the Selection(s)
Choose from the following resources to teach the selection(s):
_____   During Reading, *SE/ATE*, pp. 192–197
_____   Writing Skills: Character Sketch, *ATE*, p. 195
_____   Speaking & Listening Skills: Define Group Roles, *ATE*, p. 197
_____   Compare Literature: Tone, *Meeting the Standards Unit 2*, p. 55

Differentiate Instruction
Consider the following alternative teaching options to differentiate instruction:
_____   Reading Proficiency, *ATE*, p. 193
_____   Kinesthetic Learning, *ATE*, p. 193
_____   Visual Learning, *ATE*, p. 194
_____   Enrichment, *ATE*, p. 196
_____   Reading Strategies and Skills: Make Predictions, *Differentiated Instruction for Developing Readers,* pp. 16–18
_____   Identifying Main Ideas, *Differentiated Instruction for English Language Learners,* pp. 64–69

After Reading

Review and Extend

Use the following materials to review and extend the lesson:

_____ After Reading, *SE/ATE*, pp. 196, 198

_____ Compare Literature: Theme, *Meeting the Standards Unit 2*, p. 57

_____ Make Connections, *Meeting the Standards Unit 2*, p. 58

_____ What Do You Think? *Meeting the Standards Unit 2*, p. 61

_____ Possessive Pronouns, *Exceeding the Standards: Grammar & Style*, pp. 43–45

_____ Descriptive Writing: Describe a Dreamlike Atmosphere, *Exceeding the Standards: Grammar & Style*, pp. 7–13

Assess

Administer the following assessment tool(s):

_____ Selection Quiz: Focus on "Jed's Grandfather," *Meeting the Standards Unit 2*, p. 59

_____ Selection Quiz: Focus on "The Courage That My Mother Had," *Meeting the Standards Unit 2*, p. 60

_____ Lesson Test, *Assessment Guide*, pp. 67–69

Technology Tools

Enhance the lesson with interactive activities offered in these technology supplements:

- EMC Launchpad
- Annotated Teacher's Edition on CD
- Interactive Student Text on CD
- Exam*View*® Assessment Suite on CD
- Visual Teaching Package
- ETS Online Criterion-Based Essay Grader (Grades 9–12)
- EMC Audio Library
- EMC E-Library
- **mirrorsandwindows.com**

Name: _____ Date: _____

M   T   W   Th   F

Antaeus / in the inner city, p. 199

Directed Reading
- **Reading Level:** Moderate
- **Difficulty Consideration:** Vocabulary
- **Ease Factor:** Interesting plot

Pacing
- **Regular Schedule:** 3 days
- **Block Schedule:** 1.5 days

Objectives
Studying this lesson will enable students to
- use reading skills such as context clues
- define conflict and recognize how causes and effects reveal a story's main conflict
- describe the literary accomplishments of Borden Deal and how his family history influenced his writing
- appreciate a story that contains a literary allusion

Before Reading

Preview and Motivate
Choose from the following materials to preview the lesson and motivate your students:
_____ Before Reading, *SE/ATE*, p. 199
_____ Practice Vocabulary, *Meeting the Standards Unit 2*, p. 62

During Reading

Teach the Selection(s)
Choose from the following resources to teach the selection(s):
_____ During Reading, *SE/ATE*, pp. 200–209
_____ History Connection: Victory Gardens, *SE/ATE*, p. 203
_____ Literature Connection: "in the inner city," *SE/ATE*, p. 210
_____ Grammar Skills: Coordinating Conjunctions, *ATE*, p. 203
_____ Vocabulary Skills: Find Pronunciations, *ATE*, p. 204
_____ Research Skills: Identify a Contemporary Topic, *ATE*, p. 205
_____ Reading Skills: Clarify, *ATE*, pp. 207, 209
_____ Use Reading Skills: Use Context Clues, *Meeting the Standards Unit 2*, p. 63
_____ Analyze Literature: Conflict, *Meeting the Standards Unit 2*, p. 64
_____ Use Reading Skills: Analyze Cause and Effect, *Meeting the Standards Unit 2*, p. 65

Differentiate Instruction
Consider the following alternative teaching options to differentiate instruction:
_____ Reading Proficiency, *ATE*, pp. 201, 210
_____ English Language Learning, *ATE*, p. 202
_____ Visual Learning, *ATE*, p. 206
_____ Kinesthetic Learning, *ATE*, p. 206
_____ Enrichment, *ATE*, p. 208
_____ Fiction and Poetry Analysis: Comparing Character and Speaker, *Differentiated Instruction for Advanced Students*, p. 12
_____ Use Context Clues, *Differentiated Instruction for English Language Learners*, pp. 70–85

After Reading

Review and Extend

Use the following materials to review and extend the lesson:

_____ After Reading, *SE/ATE*, pp. 209, 211

_____ Expository Writing: Compare-and-Contrast Essay, *Meeting the Standards Unit 2*, p. 66

_____ Critical Literacy: Explore an Allusion, *Exceeding the Standards: Extension Activities*, p. 7

_____ Pronouns, *Exceeding the Standards: Grammar & Style*, pp. 33–36

Assess

Administer the following assessment tool(s):

_____ Selection Quiz, *Meeting the Standards Unit 2*, pp. 67–68

_____ Lesson Test, *Assessment Guide*, pp. 70–72

Technology Tools

Enhance the lesson with interactive activities offered in these technology supplements:

- EMC Launchpad
- Annotated Teacher's Edition on CD
- Interactive Student Text on CD
- Exam*View*® Assessment Suite on CD
- Visual Teaching Package
- ETS Online Criterion-Based Essay Grader (Grades 9–12)
- EMC Audio Library
- EMC E-Library
- **mirrorsandwindows.com**

LESSON PLAN

Name: _____ Date: _____

M   T   W   Th   F

Seventh Grade, p. 212

Grammar & Style Workshop: Consistent Verb Tense, p. 219

Directed Reading
- **Reading Level:** Easy
- **Difficulty Consideration:** None
- **Ease Factor:** Familiar themes

Pacing
- **Regular Schedule:** 2 days
- **Block Schedule:** 1 day

Objectives
Studying this lesson will enable students to
- use reading skills such as identifying sequence of events
- define a dynamic character and recognize how the character changes in the story
- describe the work of Gary Soto and how his Mexican-American heritage influences his writing
- appreciate humor in a story about young love

Before Reading

Preview and Motivate
Choose from the following materials to preview the lesson and motivate your students:
_____ Before Reading, *SE/ATE*, p. 212
_____ Practice Vocabulary, *Meeting the Standards Unit 2*, p. 69

During Reading

Teach the Selection(s)
Choose from the following resources to teach the selection(s):
_____ During Reading, *SE/ATE*, pp. 213–217
_____ Reading Skills: Author's Perspective, *ATE*, p. 215
_____ Grammar Skills: Infinitives, *ATE*, p. 216
_____ Writing Skills: Personal Anecdotes, *ATE*, p. 217
_____ Use Reading Skills: Retell Sequence, *Meeting the Standards Unit 2*, p. 70
_____ Analyze Literature: Character, *Meeting the Standards Unit 2*, p. 71

Differentiate Instruction
Consider the following alternative teaching options to differentiate instruction:
_____ English Language Learning, *ATE*, p. 214

After Reading

Review and Extend
Use the following materials to review and extend the lesson:
_____ After Reading, *SE/ATE*, p. 218
_____ Describe and Critique: Fiction, *Meeting the Standards Unit 2*, p. 72
_____ Singular and Plural Nouns, *Exceeding the Standards: Grammar & Style*, pp. 23–24

Teach the Workshop(s)

Select from the following materials to teach the workshop(s):

_____   Grammar & Style: Consistent Verb Tense, *SE/ATE*, p. 219

_____   Language Arts Handbook Section 3.5, Verbs, *SE/ATE*, pp. 859–860

_____   Verb Tenses, *Exceeding the Standards: Grammar & Style*, pp. 61–64

_____   Maintaining Consistent Verb Tense, *Exceeding the Standards: Grammar & Style*, pp. 198–200

Assess

Administer the following assessment tool(s):

_____   Selection Quiz, *Meeting the Standards Unit 2*, p. 73

_____   Lesson Test, *Assessment Guide*, pp. 73–75

Technology Tools

Enhance the lesson with interactive activities offered in these technology supplements:

- EMC Launchpad
- Annotated Teacher's Edition on CD
- Interactive Student Text on CD
- Exam*View*® Assessment Suite on CD
- Visual Teaching Package
- ETS Online Criterion-Based Essay Grader (Grades 9–12)
- EMC Audio Library
- EMC E-Library
- **mirrorsandwindows.com**

Name: _____ Date: _____

Papa's Parrot, p. 220

Independent Reading
- **Reading Level:** Easy
- **Difficulty Consideration:** None
- **Ease Factor:** Straightforward

Pacing
- **Regular Schedule:** 1 day
- **Block Schedule:** 0.5 day

Objectives
Studying this lesson will enable students to
- read with developing fluency
- read silently with comprehension for a sustained period of time

---

Before Reading

Preview and Motivate
Choose from the following materials to preview the lesson and motivate your students:
____   Before Reading, *SE/ATE*, p. 220
____   Vocabulary, *Meeting the Standards Unit 2*, p. 74

During Reading

Teach the Selection(s)
Choose from the following resources to teach the selection(s):
____   During Reading, *SE/ATE*, pp. 220–223
____   Reading Skills: Identify Text Structure, *ATE*, p. 223
____   Identify Cause and Effect, *Meeting the Standards Unit 2*, p. 75
____   Questions to Answer as You Read, *Meeting the Standards Unit 2*, p. 76

Differentiate Instruction
Consider the following alternative teaching options to differentiate instruction:
____   Reading Proficiency, *ATE*, p. 222
____   Enrichment, *ATE*, p. 222

After Reading

Review and Extend
Use the following materials to review and extend the lesson:
____   After Reading, *SE/ATE*, p. 223
____   Make Connections, *Meeting the Standards Unit 2*, p. 78
____   Describe and Critique: Fiction, *Meeting the Standards Unit 2*, p. 79

Assess
Administer the following assessment tool(s):
____   Lesson Test, *Assessment Guide*, pp. 76–78

Technology Tools

Enhance the lesson with interactive activities offered in these technology supplements:

- EMC Launchpad
- Annotated Teacher's Edition on CD
- Interactive Student Text on CD
- Exam*View*® Assessment Suite on CD
- Visual Teaching Package

- ETS Online Criterion-Based Essay Grader (Grades 9–12)
- EMC Audio Library
- EMC E-Library
- **mirrorsandwindows.com**

Name: _____ Date: _____

M   T   W   Th   F

The Smallest Dragonboy, p. 224

Independent Reading
- **Reading Level:** Challenging
- **Difficulty Consideration:** Vocabulary and setting
- **Ease Factor:** Sympathetic main character and interesting plot

Pacing
- **Regular Schedule:** 2 days
- **Block Schedule:** 1 day

Objectives
Studying this lesson will enable students to
- read with developing fluency
- read silently with comprehension for a sustained period of time

Before Reading

Preview and Motivate
Choose from the following materials to preview the lesson and motivate your students:
_____   Before Reading, *SE/ATE*, p. 224
_____   Vocabulary, *Meeting the Standards Unit 2*, p. 81

During Reading

Teach the Selection(s)
Choose from the following resources to teach the selection(s):
_____   During Reading, *SE/ATE*, pp. 224–236
_____   Reading Skills: Take Notes, *ATE*, p. 226
_____   Reading Skills: Use Context Clues, *ATE*, p. 229
_____   Research Skills: Bibliographic Entries, *ATE*, p. 231
_____   Reading Skills: Monitor Comprehension, *ATE*, p. 233
_____   Grammar Skills: Superlative Adjectives, *ATE*, p. 235
_____   Identify Main Characters, *Meeting the Standards Unit 2*, p. 82

Differentiate Instruction
Consider the following alternative teaching options to differentiate instruction:
_____   Reading Proficiency, *ATE*, pp. 227, 228
_____   Auditory Learning, *ATE*, p. 230
_____   English Language Learning, *ATE*, p. 230
_____   Visual Learning, *ATE*, p. 232
_____   Kinesthetic Learning, *ATE*, p. 234
_____   Enrichment, *ATE*, p. 236
_____   Independent Reading Symbolism Analysis: Symbolism in Fantasy and Science Fiction, *Differentiated Instruction for Advanced Students*, p. 13

After Reading

Review and Extend

Use the following materials to review and extend the lesson:

____ After Reading, *SE/ATE*, p. 236

____ Who Said That? *Meeting the Standards Unit 2*, p. 83

____ Cross-Curriculum, *Meeting the Standards Unit 2*, p. 84

____ Describe and Critique: Fiction, *Meeting the Standards Unit 2*, p. 85

Assess

Administer the following assessment tool(s):

____ Lesson Test, *Assessment Guide*, pp. 79–81

Technology Tools

Enhance the lesson with interactive activities offered in these technology supplements:

- EMC Launchpad
- Annotated Teacher's Edition on CD
- Interactive Student Text on CD
- Exam*View*® Assessment Suite on CD
- Visual Teaching Package

- ETS Online Criterion-Based Essay Grader (Grades 9–12)
- EMC Audio Library
- EMC E-Library
- **mirrorsandwindows.com**

Name: _____ Date: _____

M T W Th F

Writing Workshop: Narrative Writing—Writing a Short Story, p. 238

Pacing
- **Regular Schedule:** 3 days
- **Block Schedule:** 1.5 days

Objectives
Participating in this lesson will help enable students to
- write a short story that develops complex, believable characters
- write a short story that has a vivid setting
- write a short story that has a logically organized plot
- write a short story that maintains one point of view

Teach the Workshop
Select from the following resources to teach the workshop:
_____   Narrative Writing: Writing a Short Story, *SE/ATE*, pp. 238–245
_____   Writing Skills: Mood, *ATE*, p. 241
_____   Writing Skills: Sensory Details, *ATE*, p. 243
_____   Speaking & Listening Skills: Choral Reading, *ATE*, p. 245
_____   Language Arts Handbook Section 4.1, The Writing Process, *SE/ATE*, pp. 888–897

Differentiate Instruction
Consider the following alternative teaching options to differentiate instruction:
_____   Reading Proficiency, *ATE*, pp. 239, 240
_____   Enrichment, *ATE*, p. 239
_____   Visual and Kinesthetic Learning, *ATE*, p. 240
_____   English Language Learning, *ATE*, pp. 242, 244

Review and Extend
Use the following materials to review and extend the lesson:
_____   Descriptive Writing: Describe a Dreamlike Atmosphere, *Exceeding the Standards: Writing*, pp. 7–13

Technology Tools
Enhance the lesson with interactive activities offered in these technology supplements:
- EMC Launchpad
- Annotated Teacher's Edition on CD
- Interactive Student Text on CD
- Exam*View*® Assessment Suite on CD
- Visual Teaching Package
- ETS Online Criterion-Based Essay Grader (Grades 9–12)
- EMC Audio Library
- EMC E-Library
- **mirrorsandwindows.com**

LESSON PLAN

Name: _____ Date: _____

Speaking & Listening Workshop: Giving and Actively Listening to Literary Presentations, p. 246

Pacing
- **Regular Schedule:** 2 days
- **Block Schedule:** 1 day

Objectives
Participating in this lesson will help enable students to
- deliver literary presentations that appeal to their audience

- deliver literary presentations that contain vivid sensory details and descriptive words
- deliver literary presentations that exhibit appropriate pacing for tone and purpose
- deliver literary presentations that engage listeners with dialogue
- deliver literary presentations that employ effective nonverbal expression

---

Teach the Workshop
Select from the following resources to teach the workshop:
_____ Speaking & Listening Workshop: Giving and Actively Listening to Literary Presentations, *SE/ATE*, pp. 246–247
_____ Language Arts Handbook Section 7.1, Verbal and Nonverbal Communication, *SE/ATE*, p. 912
_____ Language Arts Handbook Section 7.2, Listening Skills, *SE/ATE*, pp. 913–914
_____ Language Arts Handbook Section 7.7, Oral Interpretation, *SE/ATE*, pp. 917–918

Differentiate Instruction
Consider the following alternative teaching options to differentiate instruction:
_____ English Language Learning, *ATE*, p. 247
_____ Enrichment, *ATE*, p. 247

Review and Extend
Use the following materials to review and extend the lesson:
_____ Giving and Actively Listening to Literary Presentations, *Exceeding the Standards: Speaking & Listening*, pp. 4–6

Technology Tools
Enhance the lesson with interactive activities offered in these technology supplements:
- EMC Launchpad
- Annotated Teacher's Edition on CD
- Interactive Student Text on CD
- Exam*View*® Assessment Suite on CD
- Visual Teaching Package
- ETS Online Criterion-Based Essay Grader (Grades 9–12)
- EMC Audio Library
- EMC E-Library
- **mirrorsandwindows.com**

Name: _____ Date: _____

M   T   W   Th   F

Test Practice Workshop, p. 248

Pacing
- **Regular Schedule:** 1 day
- **Block Schedule:** 0.5 day

Objectives
Participating in this lesson will help enable students to
- write a literary response based on a timed writing prompt

- answer standardized test questions that demonstrate revising and editing skills
- demonstrate the ability to make inferences from a reading by answering standardized questions

Teach the Workshop
Select from the following resources to teach the workshop:
____   Writing Skills: Literary Response, *SE/ATE*, p. 248
____   Revising and Editing Skills, *SE/ATE*, p. 249
____   Reading Skills, *SE/ATE*, pp. 250–251
____   Test-Taking Skills: Eliminate Incorrect Responses, *ATE*, p. 251
____   Language Arts Handbook Section 8.1, Preparing for Tests, *SE/ATE*, p. 921
____   Language Arts Handbook Section 8.4, Answering Multiple-Choice Questions, *SE/ATE*, p. 922
____   Language Arts Handbook Section 8.5, Answering Reading Comprehension Questions, *SE/ATE*, p. 923

Differentiate Instruction
Consider the following alternative teaching options to differentiate instruction:
____   English Language Learning, *ATE*, p. 250

Review and Extend
Use the following materials to review and extend the lesson:
____   Fiction Study Guide: Practice Test, *Meeting the Standards Unit 2*, pp. 11–17
____   Literary Response Practice Test: Timed Writing, *Exceeding the Standards: Writing*, p. 7

Technology Tools
Enhance the lesson with interactive activities offered in these technology supplements:
- EMC Launchpad
- Annotated Teacher's Edition on CD
- Interactive Student Text on CD
- Exam*View*® Assessment Suite on CD
- Visual Teaching Package
- ETS Online Criterion-Based Essay Grader (Grades 9–12)
- EMC Audio Library
- EMC E-Library
- **mirrorsandwindows.com**

Name: _____   Date: _____
                                                             M   T   W   Th   F

Unit 3 Nonfiction Opener, p. 252

Pacing
- **Regular Schedule:** 1 day
- **Block Schedule:** 0.5 day

Objectives
Studying this lesson will enable students to
- connect the themes expressed in the selections to their own lives and to the world around them

- identify common forms of nonfiction
- understand different elements of nonfiction
- understand variations of literary forms and author's use of language to develop forms

Plan the Unit
Use the following resources to plan instruction for this unit:
____   Unit 3 Visual Planning Guide: Unit-Based Resources, *ATE*, pp. 252A–252B
____   Unit 3 Visual Planning Guide: Lesson-by-Lesson Resources, *ATE*, pp. 252C–252D
____   Unit 3 Scope & Sequence Guide, *ATE*, pp. 252E–252J
____   Unit 3 Building Vocabulary, *ATE*, pp. 252K–252L
____   Launch the Unit, *ATE*, p. 252

Teach the Unit Opener
Choose from the following resources to teach the unit opener:
____   Unit 3 Overview, *SE/ATE*, pp. 252–253
____   Introduction to Nonfiction, *SE/ATE*, pp. 254–255
____   Nonfiction Study Guide: Introduction to Nonfiction, *Meeting the Standards Unit 3*, pp. 1–3
____   Nonfiction Study Guide: Applying Introduction to Autobiography, Memoir, and Biography Selections, *Meeting the Standards Unit 3*, pp. 4–5
____   Nonfiction Study Guide: Master Vocabulary List, *Meeting the Standards Unit 3*, p. 17

Differentiate Instruction
Consider the following alternative teaching options to differentiate instruction:
____   Reading Proficiency, *ATE*, p. 255
____   Enrichment, *ATE*, p. 255

Extend the Unit
Choose from the following resources to extend the unit:
____   For Your Reading List, *SE/ATE*, p. 361
____   Unit 3, *Exceeding the Standards: Grammar & Style*, pp. 49–81
____   Distinguish Between Fiction and Nonfiction, *Exceeding the Standards: Literature & Reading*, pp. 6–7
____   Lifelong Learning: Analyzing Yourself: Part 1, *Exceeding the Standards: Special Topics*, pp. 10–11
____   Media Literacy: Using PowerPoint, *Exceeding the Standards: Special Topics*, pp. 12–13
____   Unit 3, *Exceeding the Standards: Vocabulary & Spelling*, pp. 21–34

Assess

Administer the following assessment tool(s):

_____ Formative Surveys 1 and 2, *Assessment Guide*, pp. 3–20

_____ Reading Fluency Assessments, Passages 1 and 2, *Assessment Guide*, pp. 297–298

_____ Unit 3 Exam, *Assessment Guide*, pp. 261–264

Technology Tools

Enhance the lesson with interactive activities offered in these technology supplements:

- EMC Launchpad
- Annotated Teacher's Edition on CD
- Interactive Student Text on CD
- Exam*View*® Assessment Suite on CD
- Visual Teaching Package
- ETS Online Criterion-Based Essay Grader (Grades 9–12)
- EMC Audio Library
- EMC E-Library
- **mirrorsandwindows.com**

Name: _____   Date: _____

from **An American Childhood**, p. 257

Grammar & Style Workshop: Phrases, p. 264

Guided Reading: Reading Model
- **Reading Level:** Challenging
- **Difficulty Consideration:** Vocabulary and style
- **Ease Factor:** Sympathetic narrator

Pacing
- **Regular Schedule:** 2 days
- **Block Schedule:** 1 day

Objectives
Studying this lesson will enable students to
- use reading skills such as context clues
- define autobiography and memoir and recognize how this selection is an example of those genres
- describe the influence books and reading had on Annie Dillard
- appreciate how childhood experiences helped shape a writer

Before Reading

Preview and Motivate
Choose from the following materials to preview the lesson and motivate your students:
____   Nonfiction Reading Model, *SE/ATE*, p. 256
____   Before Reading, *SE/ATE*, p. 257
____   How to Read Nonfiction, *Meeting the Standards Unit 3*, p. 19
____   Vocabulary, *Meeting the Standards Unit 3*, p. 21
____   Make Connections, *Meeting the Standards Unit 3*, p. 22

During Reading

Teach the Selection(s)
Choose from the following resources to teach the selection(s):
____   During Reading, *SE/ATE*, pp. 258–262
____   Reading Skills: Compare and Contrast, *ATE*, p. 259
____   Writing Skills: Supporting Details, *ATE*, p. 261
____   Use Reading Skills: Make Inferences, *Meeting the Standards Unit 3*, p. 23

Differentiate Instruction
Consider the following alternative teaching options to differentiate instruction:
____   Reading Proficiency, *ATE*, p. 260
____   Visual Learning, *ATE*, p. 260
____   English Language Learning, *ATE*, p. 262
____   Enrichment, *ATE*, p. 262
____   Reading Strategies and Skills Practice: Unlock Word Meaning, *Differentiated Instruction for Developing Readers*, pp. 19–21
____   Memoir Writing Assignment: Write and Record a Memoir, *Differentiated Instruction for Advanced Students*, pp. 14–15

After Reading

Review and Extend

Use the following materials to review and extend the lesson:

_____ After Reading, *SE/ATE*, p. 263

_____ Analyze Literature: Autobiography and Memoir, *Meeting the Standards Unit 3*, p. 24

_____ Verb Tenses, *Exceeding the Standards: Grammar & Style*, pp. 61–64

Teach the Workshop(s)

Select from the following materials to teach the workshop(s):

_____ Grammar & Style: Phrases, *SE/ATE*, p. 264

_____ Language Arts Handbook Section 3.11, Phrases, *SE/ATE*, pp. 866–867

_____ Phrases and Clauses, *Exceeding the Standards: Grammar & Style*, pp. 132–133

_____ Prepositional Phrases, *Exceeding the Standards: Grammar & Style*, pp. 134–136

_____ Verbal Phrases, *Exceeding the Standards: Grammar & Style*, pp. 137–139

_____ Appositive Phrases, *Exceeding the Standards: Grammar & Style*, pp. 140–143

Assess

Administer the following assessment tool(s):

_____ Selection Quiz, *Meeting the Standards Unit 3*, pp. 25–26

_____ Lesson Test, *Assessment Guide*, pp. 82–84

Technology Tools

Enhance the lesson with interactive activities offered in these technology supplements:

- EMC Launchpad
- Annotated Teacher's Edition on CD
- Interactive Student Text on CD
- Exam*View*® Assessment Suite on CD
- Visual Teaching Package
- ETS Online Criterion-Based Essay Grader (Grades 9–12)
- EMC Audio Library
- EMC E-Library
- **mirrorsandwindows.com**

Name: _____ Date: _____

Elizabeth I, p. 265

Vocabulary & Spelling Workshop: Greek, Latin, and Anglo-Saxon Roots, p. 280

Guided Reading: Reading Model
- **Reading Level:** Moderate
- **Difficulty Consideration:** Vocabulary
- **Ease Factor:** Opening paragraph

Pacing
- **Regular Schedule:** 4 days
- **Block Schedule:** 2 days

Objectives

Studying this lesson will enable students to
- use reading skills such as distinguishing fact from opinion
- define biography and study an example of the form
- explore biographer Milton Meltzer's treatment of a major historical figure in conjunction with some of the subject's own writing
- appreciate the life of a person who played a pivotal role in history

---

Before Reading

Preview and Motivate

Choose from the following materials to preview the lesson and motivate your students:
____   Nonfiction Reading Model, *SE/ATE*, p. 256
____   Before Reading, *SE/ATE*, p. 265
____   Vocabulary, *Meeting the Standards Unit 3*, p. 27
____   Set Purpose, *Meeting the Standards Unit 3*, p. 28

During Reading

Teach the Selection(s)

Choose from the following resources to teach the selection(s):
____   During Reading, *SE/ATE*, pp. 266–276
____   Cultural Connection: The Renaissance, *SE/ATE*, p. 272
____   Primary Source Connection: Writings by Queen Elizabeth I, *SE/ATE*, pp. 277–278
____   Reading Skills: Distinguish Face from Opinion, *ATE*, p. 269
____   Grammar Skills: Interrupters, *ATE*, p. 271
____   Grammar Skills: Participles, *ATE*, p. 273
____   Grammar Skills: Participles and Gerunds, *ATE*, p. 275
____   Use Reading Skills: Distinguish Fact from Opinion, *Meeting the Standards Unit 3*, p. 29
____   Analyze Literature: Time and Sequence, *Meeting the Standards Unit 3*, p. 30

Differentiate Instruction

Consider the following alternative teaching options to differentiate instruction:

_____ English Language Learning, *ATE*, p. 267

_____ Enrichment, *ATE*, pp. 268, 270, 274, 278

_____ Reading Proficiency, *ATE*, p. 268

_____ Enrichment and Visual Learning, *ATE*, p. 272

_____ Kinesthetic Learning, *ATE*, p. 276

_____ Reading Strategies and Skills Practice: Use Text Organization, *Differentiated Instruction for Developing Readers*, pp. 22–24

After Reading

Review and Extend

Use the following materials to review and extend the lesson:

_____ After Reading, *SE/ATE*, pp. 276, 279

_____ Analyze Nonfiction: Pros and Cons, *Meeting the Standards Unit 3*, p. 31

_____ Analyze Nonfiction: Pros and Cons, *Exceeding the Standards: Grammar & Style*, pp. 75–78

Teach the Workshop(s)

Select from the following materials to teach the workshop(s):

_____ Vocabulary & Spelling: Greek, Latin, and Anglo-Saxon Roots, *SE/ATE*, p. 280

_____ Language Arts Handbook Section 2.2, Breaking Words into Base Words, Word Roots, Prefixes, and Suffixes, *SE/ATE*, pp. 837–840

_____ Greek and Latin Roots, *Exceeding the Standards: Vocabulary & Style*, pp. 55–56

Assess

Administer the following assessment tool(s):

_____ Selection Quiz, *Meeting the Standards Unit 3*, pp. 32–33

_____ Lesson Test, *Assessment Guide*, pp. 85–87

Technology Tools

Enhance the lesson with interactive activities offered in these technology supplements:

- EMC Launchpad
- Annotated Teacher's Edition on CD
- Interactive Student Text on CD
- Exam*View*® Assessment Suite on CD
- Visual Teaching Package

- ETS Online Criterion-Based Essay Grader (Grades 9–12)
- EMC Audio Library
- EMC E-Library
- **mirrorsandwindows.com**

LESSON PLAN

Name: _____   Date: _____

                                                              M   T   W   Th   F

Literary Element: Understanding the Essay, p. 281

Names/Nombres / Face It, p. 282

Guided Reading: Reading Model
- **Reading Level:** Moderate
- **Difficulty Consideration:** Footnotes and vocabulary
- **Ease Factor:** Length

Pacing
- **Regular Schedule:** 3 days
- **Block Schedule:** 1.5 days

Objectives
Studying this lesson will enable students to
- use reading skills such as identifying the author's purpose
- define personal essay and recognize an example of the genre
- describe the literary accomplishments of Julia Alvarez
- appreciate a story about the experience of coming to the United States from another country

---

Before Reading

Teach the Feature(s)
Select from the following resources to teach the feature(s):
_____ Literary Element: Understanding the Essay, *SE/ATE*, p. 281
_____ Nonfiction Study Guide: Understanding the Essay and Applying the Essay to the Selections, *Meeting the Standards Unit 3*, pp. 6–10

Preview and Motivate
Choose from the following materials to preview the lesson and motivate your students:
_____ Nonfiction Reading Model, *SE/ATE*, p. 256
_____ Before Reading, *SE/ATE*, p. 282
_____ Set Purpose and Vocabulary and Spelling Practice, *Meeting the Standards Unit 3*, pp. 34–35
_____ Use Reading Skills: Identify Author's Purpose, *Meeting the Standards Unit 3*, p. 36

During Reading

Teach the Selection(s)
Choose from the following resources to teach the selection(s):
_____ During Reading, *SE/ATE*, pp. 283–288
_____ Geography Connection: The Dominican Republic, *SE/ATE*, p. 285
_____ Literature Connection: "Face It," *SE/ATE*, p. 289
_____ Reading Skills: Identify Author's Purpose, *ATE*, p. 285
_____ Grammar Skills: Compound and Complex Sentences, *ATE*, p. 287
_____ Reading Skills: Make Inferences, *ATE*, p. 289

Differentiate Instruction

Consider the following alternative teaching options to differentiate instruction:

____ Auditory Learning, *ATE*, p. 284
____ Enrichment, *ATE*, p. 284
____ Reading Proficiency, *ATE*, p. 286
____ English Language Learning, *ATE*, p. 288
____ Comparing Literature Activity: Comparing Theme and Narrator Through Dialogue, *Differentiated Instruction for Advanced Students*, p. 16
____ Identify Author's Purpose, *Differentiated Instruction for English Language Learners*, pp. 86–95

After Reading

Review and Extend

Use the following materials to review and extend the lesson:

____ After Reading, *SE/ATE*, pp. 288, 290
____ Practice Vocabulary, *Meeting the Standards Unit 3*, p. 37
____ Use Reading Skills: Compare and Contrast, *Meeting the Standards Unit 3*, p. 38

Assess

Administer the following assessment tool(s):

____ Selection Quiz, *Meeting the Standards Unit 3*, pp. 39–40
____ Lesson Test, *Assessment Guide*, pp. 88–90

Technology Tools

Enhance the lesson with interactive activities offered in these technology supplements:

- EMC Launchpad
- Annotated Teacher's Edition on CD
- Interactive Student Text on CD
- Exam*View*® Assessment Suite on CD
- Visual Teaching Package
- ETS Online Criterion-Based Essay Grader (Grades 9–12)
- EMC Audio Library
- EMC E-Library
- **mirrorsandwindows.com**

Name: _____   Date: _____

M   T   W   Th   F

The Eternal Frontier, p. 291

Grammar & Style Workshop: Sentence Types, p. 296

Guided Reading: Reading Model
- **Reading Level:** Moderate
- **Difficulty Consideration:** Abstract ideas
- **Ease Factor:** Length

Pacing
- **Regular Schedule:** 2 days
- **Block Schedule:** 1 day

Objectives

Studying this lesson will enable students to
- use reading skills such as analyzing the main idea and supporting details to assess a persuasive argument
- define persuasive essay and study an example
- describe the literary accomplishments of Louis L'Amour
- appreciate an author's assessment of what humankind's future will be

---

Before Reading

Preview and Motivate

Choose from the following materials to preview the lesson and motivate your students:

____   Nonfiction Reading Model, *SE/ATE*, p. 256

____   Before Reading, *SE/ATE*, p. 291

____   Vocabulary, *Meeting the Standards Unit 3*, p. 41

____   Set Purpose, *Meeting the Standards Unit 3*, p. 42

During Reading

Teach the Selection(s)

Choose from the following resources to teach the selection(s):

____   During Reading, *SE/ATE*, pp. 292–294

____   Analyze Literature: Persuasive Essay, *Meeting the Standards Unit 3*, p. 43

Differentiate Instruction

Consider the following alternative teaching options to differentiate instruction:

____   Reading Proficiency, *ATE*, p. 293

____   Enrichment, *ATE*, p. 293

____   English Language Learning, *ATE*, p. 294

____   Kinesthetic Learning, *ATE*, p. 294

After Reading

Review and Extend

Use the following materials to review and extend the lesson:

____   After Reading, *SE/ATE*, p. 295

____   Analyze Literature: Nonfiction, *Meeting the Standards Unit 3*, p. 44

____   Collaborative Learning: Identify Facts and Opinions, *Exceeding the Standards: Extension Activities*, p. 8

____   Linking and Helping Verbs, *Exceeding the Standards: Grammar & Style*, pp. 52–57

Teach the Workshop(s)

Select from the following materials to teach the workshop(s):

_____ Grammar & Style Workshop: Sentence Types, *SE/ATE*, p. 296

_____ Language Arts Handbook Section 3.1, The Sentence, *SE/ATE*, pp. 852–854

_____ The Sentence and Its Functions, *Exceeding the Standards: Grammar & Style*, pp. 1–6

Assess

Administer the following assessment tool(s):

_____ Selection Quiz, *Meeting the Standards Unit 3*, pp. 45–46

_____ Lesson Test, *Assessment Guide*, pp. 91–93

Technology Tools

Enhance the lesson with interactive activities offered in these technology supplements:

- EMC Launchpad
- Annotated Teacher's Edition on CD
- Interactive Student Text on CD
- Exam*View*® Assessment Suite on CD
- Visual Teaching Package
- ETS Online Criterion-Based Essay Grader (Grades 9–12)
- EMC Audio Library
- EMC E-Library
- **mirrorsandwindows.com**

Name: _____   Date: _____
                                                  M   T   W   Th   F

from Off the Court / A Black Athlete Looks at Education, p. 297

Directed Reading
- **Reading Level:** Challenging
- **Difficulty Consideration:** Length and vocabulary
- **Ease Factor:** Style

Pacing
- **Regular Schedule:** 3 days
- **Block Schedule:** 1.5 days

Objectives
Studying this lesson will enable students to
- use reading skills such as analyzing the author's perspective
- define description and understand how sensory detail contributes to the description
- define the athletic and literary accomplishments of Arthur Ashe
- gain understanding of the discrimination African Americans often experienced during the 1960s and of the mindset required to succeed in professional sports

Before Reading

Preview and Motivate
Choose from the following materials to preview the lesson and motivate your students:
____ Nonfiction Reading Model, *SE/ATE*, p. 256
____ Before Reading, *SE/ATE*, p. 297
____ Vocabulary, *Meeting the Standards Unit 3*, p. 47
____ Activate Prior Knowledge, *Meeting the Standards Unit 3*, p. 48

During Reading

Teach the Selection(s)
Choose from the following resources to teach the selection(s):
____ During Reading, *SE/ATE*, pp. 298–309
____ Informational Text Connection: "A Black Athlete Looks at Education," *SE/ATE*, pp. 310–311
____ Vocabulary Skills: Acronyms and Initialisms, *ATE*, p. 299
____ Writing Skills: Topic Sentences, *ATE*, p. 301
____ Grammar Skills: Single and Compound Predicates, *ATE*, p. 303
____ Reading Skills: Take Notes, *ATE*, p. 305
____ Research Skills: Key Word Searches, *ATE*, p. 307
____ Vocabulary Skills: Use Context Clues, *ATE*, p. 309
____ Use Reading Skills: Identify Main Idea, *Meeting the Standards Unit 3*, p. 49

Differentiate Instruction
Consider the following alternative teaching options to differentiate instruction:
____ Reading Proficiency, *ATE*, pp. 300, 308
____ English Language Learning, *ATE*, p. 302
____ Enrichment, *ATE*, p. 304
____ Auditory Learning, *ATE*, p. 310
____ Reading Strategies and Skills Practice: Take Notes, *Differentiated Instruction for Developing Readers*, pp. 25–27

After Reading

Review and Extend

Use the following materials to review and extend the lesson:

____ After Reading, *SE/ATE*, pp. 309, 311

____ Use Reading Skills: Cause and Effect, *Meeting the Standards Unit 3*, p. 50

____ Action Verbs and State of Being Verbs, *Exceeding the Standards: Grammar & Style*, pp. 49–51

____ Persuasive Writing: Write a Persuasive Essay, *Exceeding the Standards: Writing*, pp. 14–22

Assess

Administer the following assessment tool(s):

____ Selection Quiz, *Meeting the Standards Unit 3*, pp. 51–52

____ Lesson Test, *Assessment Guide*, pp. 94–96

Technology Tools

Enhance the lesson with interactive activities offered in these technology supplements:

- EMC Launchpad
- Annotated Teacher's Edition on CD
- Interactive Student Text on CD
- Exam*View*® Assessment Suite on CD
- Visual Teaching Package
- ETS Online Criterion-Based Essay Grader (Grades 9–12)
- EMC Audio Library
- EMC E-Library
- **mirrorsandwindows.com**

Name: _____   Date: _____

Was Tarzan a Three-Bandage Man?, p. 312

Directed Reading
- **Reading Level:** Easy
- **Difficulty Consideration:** None
- **Ease Factor:** Humor and simple language

Pacing
- **Regular Schedule:** 1 day
- **Block Schedule:** 0.5 day

Objectives
Studying this lesson will enable students to
- use reading skills such as context clues
- define purpose and recognize the author's purpose for writing
- define the literary and comedic accomplishments of Bill Cosby
- appreciate humorous anecdotes about growing up

Before Reading

Preview and Motivate
Choose from the following materials to preview the lesson and motivate your students:
____   Before Reading, *SE/ATE*, p. 312
____   Build Background, *Meeting the Standards Unit 3*, p. 53

During Reading

Teach the Selection(s)
Choose from the following resources to teach the selection(s):
____   During Reading, *SE/ATE*, pp. 313–315
____   History Connection: Jackie Robinson, *SE/ATE*, p. 314
____   Grammar Skills: Comparative and Superlative Adjectives, *ATE*, p. 315
____   Analyze Literature: Author's Purpose, *Meeting the Standards Unit 3*, p. 54

Differentiate Instruction
Consider the following alternative teaching options to differentiate instruction:
____   Enrichment, *ATE*, p. 314
____   Kinesthetic Learning, *ATE*, p. 314
____   Biographical Research Project: A Personal Hero, *Differentiated Instruction for Advanced Students*, pp. 17–18

After Reading

Review and Extend
Use the following materials to review and extend the lesson:
____   After Reading, *SE/ATE*, p. 316
____   Expository and Creative Writing: Point of View, *Meeting the Standards Unit 3*, p. 55

Assess

Administer the following assessment tool(s):

_____ Selection Quiz, *Meeting the Standards Unit 3*, p. 56

_____ Lesson Test, *Assessment Guide*, pp. 97–99

Technology Tools

Enhance the lesson with interactive activities offered in these technology supplements:

- EMC Launchpad
- Annotated Teacher's Edition on CD
- Interactive Student Text on CD
- Exam*View*® Assessment Suite on CD
- Visual Teaching Package
- ETS Online Criterion-Based Essay Grader (Grades 9–12)
- EMC Audio Library
- EMC E-Library
- **mirrorsandwindows.com**

LESSON PLAN

Name: _____ Date: _____

M   T   W   Th   F

Fish Cheeks, p. 317

Grammar & Style Workshop: Fragments and Run-on Sentences, p. 321

Directed Reading
- **Reading Level:** Easy
- **Difficulty Consideration:** Vocabulary
- **Ease Factor:** Length

Pacing
- **Regular Schedule:** 1 day
- **Block Schedule:** 0.5 day

Objectives
Studying this lesson will enable students to
- use reading skills such as analyzing text structure
- define sensory details and explain how they enrich a story
- define the literary accomplishments of Amy Tan and explain how her Chinese-American background influences her writing
- appreciate an account of a formative learning experience

Before Reading

Preview and Motivate
Choose from the following materials to preview the lesson and motivate your students:
____ Before Reading, *SE/ATE*, p. 317
____ Set Purpose, *Meeting the Standards Unit 3*, p. 57
____ Vocabulary, *Meeting the Standards Unit 3*, p. 58

During Reading

Teach the Selection(s)
Choose from the following resources to teach the selection(s):
____ During Reading, *SE/ATE*, pp. 318–319
____ Analyze Literature: Sensory Details, *Meeting the Standards Unit 3*, p. 58

Differentiate Instruction
Consider the following alternative teaching options to differentiate instruction:
____ English Language Learning, *ATE*, p. 319
____ Enrichment, *ATE*, p. 319
____ Analyze Text Structure, *Differentiated Instruction for English Language Learners*, pp. 96–102

After Reading

Review and Extend
Use the following materials to review and extend the lesson:
____ After Reading, *SE/ATE*, p. 320
____ Use Reading Skills: Analyze Cause and Effect, *Meeting the Standards Unit 3*, p. 59
____ Transitive and Intransitive Verbs, *Exceeding the Standards: Grammar & Style*, pp. 58–60

Teach the Workshop(s)

Select from the following materials to teach the workshop(s):

_____ Grammar & Style: Fragments and Run-on Sentences, *SE/ATE*, p. 321

_____ Language Arts Handbook Section 3.17, Writing Effective Sentences, *SE/ATE*, pp. 884–887

_____ Sentence Fragments, *Exceeding the Standards: Grammar & Style*, pp. 201–203

_____ Run-On Sentences, *Exceeding the Standards: Grammar & Style*, pp. 204–206

Assess

Administer the following assessment tool(s):

_____ Selection Quiz, *Meeting the Standards Unit 3*, pp. 60–61

_____ Lesson Test, *Assessment Guide*, pp. 100–102

Technology Tools

Enhance the lesson with interactive activities offered in these technology supplements:

- EMC Launchpad
- Annotated Teacher's Edition on CD
- Interactive Student Text on CD
- Exam*View*® Assessment Suite on CD
- Visual Teaching Package
- ETS Online Criterion-Based Essay Grader (Grades 9–12)
- EMC Audio Library
- EMC E-Library
- **mirrorsandwindows.com**

LESSON PLAN

Name: _____   Date: _____

M   T   W   Th   F

A Bittersweet Memoir / Searching for January, p. 322

Directed Reading
"A Bittersweet Memoir"
- **Reading Level:** Moderate
- **Difficulty Consideration:** Length
- **Ease Factor:** Vocabulary

"Searching for January"
- **Reading Level:** Moderate
- **Difficulty Consideration:** Unfamiliar subject
- **Ease Factor:** Conversational tone

Pacing
- **Regular Schedule:** 3 days
- **Block Schedule:** 1.5 days

Objectives
Studying this lesson will enable students to
- compare literary selections of different genres
- use reading skills such as analyzing the author's perspective
- define characterization and learn to recognize both direct and indirect forms of characterization
- explore and compare the tributes to Roberto Clemente created by a biographer and a fiction writer
- enjoy two portrayals of a noted baseball player

Before Reading

Preview and Motivate
Choose from the following materials to preview the lesson and motivate your students:
_____ Before Reading, *SE/ATE*, p. 322
_____ Build Background, Set Purpose, and Practice Vocabulary, *Meeting the Standards Unit 3*, p. 62

During Reading

Teach the Selection(s)
Choose from the following resources to teach the selection(s):
_____ During Reading, *SE/ATE*, pp. 323–338
_____ Research Skills: Find Images, *ATE*, p. 325
_____ Grammar Skills: Adjective Phrases and Clauses, *ATE*, p. 327
_____ Vocabulary Skills: Specialized Words, *ATE*, p. 329
_____ Writing Skills: Use References, *ATE*, p. 331
_____ Writing Skills: Monologue, *ATE*, p. 335
_____ Writing Skills: Audience, *ATE*, p. 337
_____ Compare Literature, *Meeting the Standards Unit 3*, p. 63

Differentiate Instruction
Consider the following alternative teaching options to differentiate instruction:
_____ English Language Learning, *ATE*, pp. 324, 330
_____ Reading Proficiency, *ATE*, p. 326
_____ Enrichment, *ATE*, pp. 328, 338
_____ Visual Learning, *ATE*, p. 334
_____ Auditory and Kinesthetic Learning, *ATE*, p. 336
_____ Understand Literary Elements: Characterization, *Differentiated Instruction for English Language Learners*, pp. 103–119

After Reading

Review and Extend

Use the following materials to review and extend the lesson:

____   After Reading, *SE/ATE*, pp. 332, 339

____   Compare Literature: Characterization (continued), *Meeting the Standards Unit 3*, p. 64

____   Compare Literature: Literary Elements, *Meeting the Standards Unit 3*, p. 65

____   Make Connections, *Meeting the Standards Unit 3*, p. 66

____   What Do You Think? *Meeting the Standards Unit 3*, p. 70

____   Linking and Helping Verbs, *Exceeding the Standards: Grammar & Style*, pp. 52–57

Assess

Administer the following assessment tool(s):

____   Selection Quiz: Focus on "A Bittersweet Memoir," *Meeting the Standards Unit 3*, p. 67

____   Selection Quiz: Focus on "Searching for January," *Meeting the Standards Unit 3*, pp. 68–69

____   Lesson Test, *Assessment Guide*, pp. 103–105

Technology Tools

Enhance the lesson with interactive activities offered in these technology supplements:

- EMC Launchpad
- Annotated Teacher's Edition on CD
- Interactive Student Text on CD
- Exam*View*® Assessment Suite on CD
- Visual Teaching Package
- ETS Online Criterion-Based Essay Grader (Grades 9–12)
- EMC Audio Library
- EMC E-Library
- **mirrorsandwindows.com**

Name: _____   Date: _____

M   T   W   Th   F

Madam C. J. Walker / The Sunflower Quilting Bee at Arles, p. 340

Directed Reading
- **Reading Level:** Challenging
- **Difficulty Consideration:** Vocabulary
- **Ease Factor:** Introduction

Pacing
- **Regular Schedule:** 3 days
- **Block Schedule:** 1.5 days

Objectives
Studying this lesson will enable students to
- use reading skills such as context clues
- identify the purposes of introductions and conclusions
- recognize how writers and artists keep alive the stories of people from history
- appreciate a story about how a person won freedom

Before Reading

Preview and Motivate
Choose from the following materials to preview the lesson and motivate your students:
_____ Before Reading, *SE/ATE*, p. 340
_____ Make Connections, *Meeting the Standards Unit 3*, p. 71
_____ Vocabulary, *Meeting the Standards Unit 3*, p. 72

During Reading

Teach the Selection(s)
Choose from the following resources to teach the selection(s):
_____ During Reading, *SE/ATE*, pp. 341–347
_____ Literature Connection: "The Sunflower Quilting Bee at Arles," *SE/ATE*, pp. 348–350
_____ Research Skills: Primary and Secondary Sources, *ATE*, p. 343
_____ Vocabulary Skills: Restatements, *ATE*, p. 345
_____ Grammar Skills: Independent Clauses, *ATE*, p. 347
_____ Reading Skills: Identify the Main Idea and Supporting Details, *ATE*, p. 349
_____ Use Reading Skills: Take Notes, *Meeting the Standards Unit 3*, p. 73

Differentiate Instruction
Consider the following alternative teaching options to differentiate instruction:
_____ Reading Proficiency, *ATE*, pp. 342, 346, 348
_____ Visual Learning, *ATE*, p. 342
_____ Auditory Learning, *ATE*, p. 344
_____ Enrichment, *ATE*, pp. 344, 350
_____ English Language Learning, *ATE*, p. 346
_____ Use Context Clues, *Differentiated Instruction for English Language Learners*, pp. 120–131

After Reading

Review and Extend

Use the following materials to review and extend the lesson:

____ After Reading, *SE/ATE*, pp. 347, 351

____ Analyze Literature: Characterization, *Meeting the Standards Unit 3*, p. 74

____ History Connection, *Meeting the Standards Unit 3*, pp. 75–79

____ Media Literacy: Analyze Advertisements, *Exceeding the Standards: Extension Activities,* pp. 9–10

____ Irregular Verbs, *Exceeding the Standards: Grammar & Style,* pp. 68–71

Assess

Administer the following assessment tool(s):

____ Selection Quiz, *Meeting the Standards Unit 3*, pp. 80–81

____ Lesson Test, *Assessment Guide*, pp. 106–108

Technology Tools

Enhance the lesson with interactive activities offered in these technology supplements:

- EMC Launchpad
- Annotated Teacher's Edition on CD
- Interactive Student Text on CD
- Exam*View*® Assessment Suite on CD
- Visual Teaching Package
- ETS Online Criterion-Based Essay Grader (Grades 9–12)
- EMC Audio Library
- EMC E-Library
- **mirrorsandwindows.com**

Name: _____ Date: _____

from Barrio Boy, p. 352

Independent Reading
- **Reading Level:** Moderate
- **Difficulty Consideration:** Vocabulary and metaphors
- **Ease Factor:** Sympathetic narrator

Pacing
- **Regular Schedule:** 1 day
- **Block Schedule:** 0.5 day

Objectives
Studying this lesson will enable students to
- read with developing fluency
- read silently with comprehension for a sustained period of time

---

Before Reading

Preview and Motivate
Choose from the following materials to preview the lesson and motivate your students:
_____ Before Reading, *SE/ATE*, p. 352

During Reading

Teach the Selection(s)
Choose from the following resources to teach the selection(s):
_____ During Reading, *SE/ATE*, pp. 352–355
_____ Writing Skills: Personal Narrative, *ATE*, p. 355
_____ Analyze Literature: Characterization, *Meeting the Standards Unit 3*, p. 82
_____ Make Connections, *Meeting the Standards Unit 3*, p. 83

Differentiate Instruction
Consider the following alternative teaching options to differentiate instruction:
_____ Reading Proficiency, *ATE*, p. 354
_____ Enrichment, *ATE*, p. 354

After Reading

Review and Extend
Use the following materials to review and extend the lesson:
_____ After Reading, *SE/ATE*, p. 355
_____ Practice Vocabulary, *Meeting the Standards Unit 3*, p. 84
_____ Describe and Critique: Nonfiction, *Meeting the Standards Unit 3*, pp. 87–88

Assess
Administer the following assessment tool(s):
_____ Selection Quiz, *Meeting the Standards Unit 3*, pp. 85–86
_____ Lesson Test, *Assessment Guide*, pp. 109–111

Technology Tools

Enhance the lesson with interactive activities offered in these technology supplements:

- EMC Launchpad
- Annotated Teacher's Edition on CD
- Interactive Student Text on CD
- Exam*View*® Assessment Suite on CD
- Visual Teaching Package
- ETS Online Criterion-Based Essay Grader (Grades 9–12)
- EMC Audio Library
- EMC E-Library
- **mirrorsandwindows.com**

Name: _____ Date: _____

The Night the Bed Fell, p. 356

Independent Reading
- **Reading Level:** Moderate
- **Difficulty Consideration:** Vocabulary and organization
- **Ease Factor:** Humor

Pacing
- **Regular Schedule:** 1 day
- **Block Schedule:** 0.5 day

Objectives
Studying this lesson will enable students to
- read with developing fluency
- read silently with comprehension for a sustained period of time

---

Before Reading

Preview and Motivate
Choose from the following materials to preview the lesson and motivate your students:
_____ Before Reading, *SE/ATE*, p. 356
_____ Practice Vocabulary, *Meeting the Standards Unit 3*, p. 89

During Reading

Teach the Selection(s)
Choose from the following resources to teach the selection(s):
_____ During Reading, *SE/ATE*, pp. 356–360
_____ Writing Skills: Keep a Journal, *ATE*, p. 359
_____ During Reading Questions, *Meeting the Standards Unit 3*, p. 90
_____ Text Connections: Text-to-Text, *Meeting the Standards Unit 3*, p. 91

Differentiate Instruction
Consider the following alternative teaching options to differentiate instruction:
_____ Reading Proficiency, *ATE*, p. 358
_____ English Language Learning, *ATE*, p. 358
_____ Enrichment, *ATE*, p. 360
_____ Independent Author Study: James Thurber, *Differentiated Instruction for Advanced Students*, pp. 19–20

After Reading

Review and Extend
Use the following materials to review and extend the lesson:
_____ After Reading, *SE/ATE*, p. 360
_____ Describe and Critique: Nonfiction, *Meeting the Standards Unit 3*, pp. 93–94

Assess

Administer the following assessment tool(s):

_____ Selection Quiz, *Meeting the Standards Unit 3*, p. 92

_____ Lesson Test, *Assessment Guide*, pp. 112–114

Technology Tools

Enhance the lesson with interactive activities offered in these technology supplements:

- EMC Launchpad
- Annotated Teacher's Edition on CD
- Interactive Student Text on CD
- Exam*View*® Assessment Suite on CD
- Visual Teaching Package
- ETS Online Criterion-Based Essay Grader (Grades 9–12)
- EMC Audio Library
- EMC E-Library
- **mirrorsandwindows.com**

Name: _____   Date: _____

Writing Workshop: Expository Writing—Cause-and-Effect Essay, p. 362

Pacing
- **Regular Schedule:** 3 days
- **Block Schedule:** 1.5 days

Objectives
Participating in this lesson will help enable students to
- write a cause-and-effect essay that has an interesting introduction with a clear thesis statement
- write a cause-and-effect essay that has a clear organizational pattern

- write a cause-and-effect essay that explains the relationship between effects and causes and uses cause-effect signal words and phrases
- write a cause-and-effect essay that uses details, facts, and examples to support explanations
- write a cause-and-effect essay that has a strong conclusion that sums up main points and restates the thesis

Teach the Workshop
Select from the following resources to teach the workshop:
_____   Expository Writing: Cause-and-Effect Essay, *SE/ATE*, pp. 362–367
_____   Writing Skills: Facts, Details, and Examples, *ATE*, p. 365
_____   Writing Skills: Jargon, *ATE*, p. 367
_____   Language Arts Handbook Section 4.1, The Writing Process, *SE/ATE*, pp. 888–897
_____   Language Arts Handbook Section 4.2, Modes and Purposes of Writing, *SE/ATE*, p. 897

Differentiate Instruction
Consider the following alternative teaching options to differentiate instruction:
_____   English Language Learning, *ATE*, pp. 363, 366
_____   Reading Proficiency, *ATE*, pp. 363, 364
_____   Auditory Learning, *ATE*, p. 366

Review and Extend
Use the following materials to review and extend the lesson:
_____   Persuasive Writing: Write a Persuasive Essay, *Exceeding the Standards: Writing*, pp. 14–22

Technology Tools
Enhance the lesson with interactive activities offered in these technology supplements:
- EMC Launchpad
- Annotated Teacher's Edition on CD
- Interactive Student Text on CD
- Exam*View*® Assessment Suite on CD
- Visual Teaching Package

- ETS Online Criterion-Based Essay Grader (Grades 9–12)
- EMC Audio Library
- EMC E-Library
- **mirrorsandwindows.com**

Name: _____ Date: _____

M   T   W   Th   F

Speaking & Listening Workshop: Giving and Actively Listening to Informative Presentations, p. 368

Pacing
- **Regular Schedule:** 2 days
- **Block Schedule:** 1 day

Objectives
Participating in this lesson will help enable students to
- deliver an informative presentation with an attention-grabbing introduction and conclusion

- deliver an informative presentation with a clear organization that will appeal to a particular audience
- deliver an informative presentation with a clear, concise main idea and effective supporting details

---

Teach the Workshop
Select from the following resources to teach the workshop:

_____   Speaking & Listening Workshop: Giving and Actively Listening to Informative Presentations, *SE/ATE*, pp. 368–369

_____   Speaking & Listening Skills: Retell and Summarize, *ATE*, p. 369

_____   Language Arts Handbook Section 7.6, Public Speaking, *SE/ATE*, pp. 916–917

Review and Extend
Use the following materials to review and extend the lesson:

_____   Giving and Actively Listening to Informative Presentations, *Exceeding the Standards: Speaking & Listening*, pp. 7–9

Technology Tools
Enhance the lesson with interactive activities offered in these technology supplements:
- 🗗 EMC Launchpad
- 🌐 Annotated Teacher's Edition on CD
- 🌐 Interactive Student Text on CD
- 🌐 Exam*View*® Assessment Suite on CD
- 🖳 Visual Teaching Package

- 🗗 ETS Online Criterion-Based Essay Grader (Grades 9–12)
- 🎧 EMC Audio Library
- 🗗 EMC E-Library
- 🗗 **mirrorsandwindows.com**

Name: _____ Date: _____

M   T   W   Th   F

Test Practice Workshop, p. 370

Pacing
- **Regular Schedule:** 1 day
- **Block Schedule:** 0.5 day

Objectives
Participating in this lesson will help enable students to
- write a response to literature based on a timed writing prompt

- answer standardized test questions that demonstrate revising and editing skills
- answer standardized questions that demonstrate the ability to make inferences from a reading

Teach the Workshop
Select from the following resources to teach the workshop:

____   Writing Skills: Expository Essay, *SE/ATE*, p. 370

____   Revising and Editing Skills, *SE/ATE*, p. 371

____   Reading Skills, *SE/ATE*, pp. 372–373

____   Test-Taking Skills: Eliminate Incorrect Responses, *ATE*, p. 373

____   Language Arts Handbook Section 8.1, Preparing for Tests, *SE/ATE*, p. 921

____   Language Arts Handbook Section 8.2, Strategies for Taking Standardized Tests, *SE/ATE*, pp. 921–922

____   Language Arts Handbook Section 8.5, Answering Reading Comprehension Questions, *SE/ATE*, p. 923

____   Test-Taking Strategies and Skills, *Exceeding the Standards: Test Practice*, pp. 1–4

Differentiate Instruction
Consider the following alternative teaching options to differentiate instruction:

____   Reading Proficiency, *ATE*, p. 372

Review and Extend
Use the following materials to review and extend the lesson:

____   Nonfiction Study Guide: Practice Test, *Meeting the Standards Unit 3*, pp. 11–16

____   Expository Essay Practice Test: Revising and Editing, *Exceeding the Standards: Test Practice*, pp. 8–9

Technology Tools
Enhance the lesson with interactive activities offered in these technology supplements:

- EMC Launchpad
- Annotated Teacher's Edition on CD
- Interactive Student Text on CD
- Exam*View*® Assessment Suite on CD
- Visual Teaching Package

- ETS Online Criterion-Based Essay Grader (Grades 9–12)
- EMC Audio Library
- EMC E-Library
- **mirrorsandwindows.com**

Name: _____ Date: _____

Unit 4 Nonfiction Opener, p. 374

Pacing
- **Regular Schedule:** 1 day
- **Block Schedule:** 0.5 day

Objectives
Studying this lesson will enable students to
- connect a theme expressed in a selection to their own lives
- identify common forms of nonfiction
- identify types of visual media

Plan the Unit
Use the following resources to plan instruction for this unit:

_____ Unit 4 Visual Planning Guide: Unit-Based Resources, *ATE*, pp. 374A–374B

_____ Unit 4 Visual Planning Guide: Lesson-by-Lesson Resources, *ATE*, pp. 374C–374D

_____ Unit 4 Scope & Sequence Guide, *ATE*, pp. 374E–374H

_____ Unit 4 Building Vocabulary, *ATE*, pp. 374I–374J

_____ Launch the Unit, *ATE*, p. 374

Teach the Unit Opener
Choose from the following resources to teach the unit opener:

_____ Unit 4 Overview, *SE/ATE*, pp. 374–375

_____ Introduction to Informational Text and Visual Media, *SE/ATE*, pp. 376–377

_____ Speaking & Listening Skills: Brainstorm Issues, Arguments, and Positions, *ATE*, p. 377

_____ Nonfiction Study Guide: Introduction, *Meeting the Standards Unit 4*, p. 1

_____ Nonfiction Study Guide: Understanding Informational Text and Visual Media and Applying Informational Text and Visual Media to the Selections, *Meeting the Standards Unit 4*, pp. 2–10

_____ Nonfiction Study Guide: Master Vocabulary List, *Meeting the Standards Unit 4*, p. 17

Extend the Unit
Choose from the following resources to extend the unit:

_____ For Your Reading List, *SE/ATE*, p. 447

_____ Unit 4, *Exceeding the Standards: Grammar & Style*, pp. 82–112

_____ Analyze and Interpret Informational Text and Visual Media, *Exceeding the Standards: Literature & Reading*, pp. 8–10

_____ Lifelong Learning: Analyzing Yourself: Part 2, *Exceeding the Standards: Special Topics*, pp. 14–15

_____ Media Literacy: Designing a Website, *Exceeding the Standards: Special Topics*, pp. 16–17

_____ Unit 4, *Exceeding the Standards: Vocabulary & Spelling*, pp. 35–46

Assess

Administer the following assessment tool(s):

____ Formative Surveys 1 and 2, *Assessment Guide*, pp. 3–20

____ Reading Fluency Assessments, Passages 1 and 2, *Assessment Guide*, pp. 299–300

____ Unit 4 Exam, *Assessment Guide*, pp. 265–268

Technology Tools

Enhance the lesson with interactive activities offered in these technology supplements:

- EMC Launchpad
- Annotated Teacher's Edition on CD
- Interactive Student Text on CD
- Exam*View*® Assessment Suite on CD
- Visual Teaching Package
- ETS Online Criterion-Based Essay Grader (Grades 9–12)
- EMC Audio Library
- EMC E-Library
- **mirrorsandwindows.com**

Name: _____ Date: _____

The Size of Things / Achieving Perspective, p. 378

Grammar & Style: Adjective and Adverb Clauses, p. 389

Guided Reading: Reading Model
- **Reading Level:** Challenging
- **Difficulty Consideration:** Concepts and vocabulary
- **Ease Factor:** Reading model

Pacing
- **Regular Schedule:** 3 days
- **Block Schedule:** 1.5 days

Objectives

Studying this lesson will enable students to
- use reading skills such as monitoring comprehension
- define informational text and recognize elements of this genre
- explain why Robert Jastrow has the expertise to write about matter
- appreciate an article about scale that helps them respond to nature

---

Before Reading

Preview and Motivate

Choose from the following materials to preview the lesson and motivate your students:

_____ Nonfiction Reading Model, *SE/ATE*, p. 256

_____ Before Reading, *SE/ATE*, p. 378

_____ Vocabulary: Words with Multiple Meanings, *Meeting the Standards Unit 4*, pp. 19–20

During Reading

Teach the Selection(s)

Choose from the following resources to teach the selection(s):

_____ During Reading, *SE/ATE*, pp. 379–385

_____ Literature Connection: "Achieving Perspective," *SE/ATE*, pp. 386–387

_____ Vocabulary Skills: Stressed and Unstressed Syllables, *ATE*, p. 381

_____ Reading Skills: Take Notes, *ATE*, p. 383

_____ Grammar Skills: Prepositional Phrases, *ATE*, p. 385

_____ Vocabulary Skills: Use a Dictionary, *ATE*, p. 387

_____ Science Connection: Nuclear Physics, *Meeting the Standards Unit 4*, p. 21

Differentiate Instruction

Consider the following alternative teaching options to differentiate instruction:

_____ Reading Proficiency, *ATE*, pp. 380, 386

_____ English Language Learning, *ATE*, p. 380

_____ Enrichment, *ATE*, p. 382

_____ Visual Learning, *ATE*, p. 384

After Reading

Review and Extend

Use the following materials to review and extend the lesson:

_____ After Reading, *SE/ATE*, pp. 385, 388

_____ Expository and Creative Writing: Analogies, *Meeting the Standards Unit 4*, p. 22

_____ Expository Writing: Compare-and-Contrast Essay, *Meeting the Standards Unit 4*, p. 23

Teach the Workshop(s)

Select from the following materials to teach the workshop(s):

_____ Grammar & Style: Adjective and Adverb Clauses, *SE/ATE*, p. 389

_____ Language Arts Handbook Section 3.8, Modifiers, *SE/ATE*, pp. 864–865

_____ Language Arts Handbook Section 3.12, Clauses, *SE/ATE*, p. 868

_____ Types of Clauses within a Sentence, *Exceeding the Standards: Grammar & Style*, pp. 144–150

Assess

Administer the following assessment tool(s):

_____ Selection Quiz, *Meeting the Standards Unit 4*, p. 24

_____ Lesson Test, *Assessment Guide*, pp. 115–117

Technology Tools

Enhance the lesson with interactive activities offered in these technology supplements:

- EMC Launchpad
- Annotated Teacher's Edition on CD
- Interactive Student Text on CD
- Exam*View*® Assessment Suite on CD
- Visual Teaching Package
- ETS Online Criterion-Based Essay Grader (Grades 9–12)
- EMC Audio Library
- EMC E-Library
- **mirrorsandwindows.com**

Name: _____ Date: _____

M   T   W   Th   F

from The Sibley Guide to Birds / *from* Wild Turkey, p. 390

Guided Reading: Reading Model
- **Reading Level:** Easy
- **Difficulty Consideration:** Vocabulary
- **Ease Factor:** Length and illustration

Pacing
- **Regular Schedule:** 2 days
- **Block Schedule:** 1 day

Objectives
Studying this lesson will enable students to
- use reading skills such as drawing conclusions
- interpret visual media
- recognize the work of David Allen Sibley and John James Audubon
- compare visual descriptions and written descriptions

Before Reading

Preview and Motivate
Choose from the following materials to preview the lesson and motivate your students:
_____   Nonfiction Reading Model, *SE/ATE*, p. 256
_____   Before Reading, *SE/ATE*, p. 390
_____   Build Background: Bird Field Guide, *Meeting the Standards Unit 4*, p. 25
_____   Vocabulary: Prefixes and Suffixes, *Meeting the Standards Unit 4*, pp. 26–27

During Reading

Teach the Selection(s)
Choose from the following resources to teach the selection(s):
_____   During Reading, *SE/ATE*, pp. 391–393
_____   Informational Text Connection: from *Wild Turkey*, *SE/ATE*, p. 394
_____   Speaking & Listening Skills: Visual Aids, *ATE*, p. 393
_____   Text-to-Text Connection, *Meeting the Standards Unit 4*, p. 28

Differentiate Instruction
Consider the following alternative teaching options to differentiate instruction:
_____   English Language Learning, *ATE*, pp. 392, 394
_____   Auditory Learning, *ATE*, p. 392
_____   Comparing Literature Activity: Field Guides, *Differentiated Instruction for Advanced Students*, pp. 21–22

After Reading

Review and Extend
Use the following materials to review and extend the lesson:
_____   After Reading, *SE/ATE*, pp. 393, 395
_____   Adjectives and Adverbs: Choosing the Correct Modifier, *Exceeding the Standards: Grammar & Style*, pp. 92–99

Assess

Administer the following assessment tool(s):

_____ Selection Quiz, *Meeting the Standards Unit 4*, p. 29

_____ Lesson Test, *Assessment Guide*, pp. 118–120

Technology Tools

Enhance the lesson with interactive activities offered in these technology supplements:

- EMC Launchpad
- Annotated Teacher's Edition on CD
- Interactive Student Text on CD
- Exam*View*® Assessment Suite on CD
- Visual Teaching Package
- ETS Online Criterion-Based Essay Grader (Grades 9–12)
- EMC Audio Library
- EMC E-Library
- **mirrorsandwindows.com**

Name: _____ Date: _____

M   T   W   Th   F

Ships in the Desert / I Am a Native of North America, p. 396

Grammar & Style Workshop: Simple and Compound Subjects, p. 407

Directed Reading
- **Reading Level:** Challenging
- **Difficulty Consideration:** Concepts, vocabulary, and sentence length
- **Ease Factor:** Vivid imagery

Pacing
- **Regular Schedule:** 3 days
- **Block Schedule:** 1.5 days

Objectives
Studying this lesson will enable students to
- use reading skills such as analyzing the main idea and supporting details
- define analogy and evaluate examples in the selection
- compare the perspectives that Al Gore and Chief Dan George hold regarding the environment
- appreciate literature that proposes solutions to a problem

Before Reading

Preview and Motivate

Choose from the following materials to preview the lesson and motivate your students:

_____ Before Reading, *SE/ATE*, p. 396

_____ Build Background: Offsetting Your Carbon Footprint, *Meeting the Standards Unit 4*, p. 30

During Reading

Teach the Selection(s)

Choose from the following resources to teach the selection(s):

_____ During Reading, *SE/ATE*, pp. 397–402

_____ Science Connection: Global Warming, *SE/ATE*, p. 400

_____ Informational Text Connection: "I Am a Native of North America," *SE/ATE*, pp. 403–405

_____ Grammar Skills: Types of Paragraphs, *ATE*, p. 399

_____ Speaking & Listening Skills: Main Ideas and Supporting Details, *ATE*, p. 401

_____ Grammar Skills: Parts of Speech, *ATE*, p. 405

_____ Use Reading Strategies: Visualize, *Meeting the Standards Unit 4*, p. 31

_____ Vocabulary: Denotation, Connotation, and Tone, *Meeting the Standards Unit 4*, p. 32

Differentiate Instruction

Consider the following alternative teaching options to differentiate instruction:

_____ Visual Learning, *ATE*, p. 398

_____ Reading Proficiency, *ATE*, pp. 398, 404

_____ Enrichment, *ATE*, p. 402

_____ Auditory Learning, *ATE*, p. 404

After Reading

Review and Extend

Use the following materials to review and extend the lesson:

_____ After Reading, *SE/ATE*, pp. 402, 406

_____ Analyze Literature: Theme, *Meeting the Standards Unit 4*, p. 33

_____ Text-to-Text Connection, *Meeting the Standards Unit 4*, p. 34

_____ Adjectives and Adverbs: Choosing the Correct Modifier, *Exceeding the Standards: Grammar & Style*, pp. 92–99

Teach the Workshop(s)

Select from the following materials to teach the workshop(s):

_____ Grammar & Style: Simple and Compound Subjects, *SE/ATE*, p. 407

_____ Simple and Complete Subjects and Predicates, *Exceeding the Standards: Grammar & Style*, pp. 10–12

_____ Compound Subjects, Compound Predicates, and Compound Sentences, *Exceeding the Standards: Grammar & Style*, pp. 13–15

Assess

Administer the following assessment tool(s):

_____ Selection Quiz, *Meeting the Standards Unit 4*, p. 35

_____ Lesson Test, *Assessment Guide*, pp. 121–123

Technology Tools

Enhance the lesson with interactive activities offered in these technology supplements:

- EMC Launchpad
- Annotated Teacher's Edition on CD
- Interactive Student Text on CD
- Exam*View*® Assessment Suite on CD
- Visual Teaching Package
- ETS Online Criterion-Based Essay Grader (Grades 9–12)
- EMC Audio Library
- EMC E-Library
- **mirrorsandwindows.com**

Name: _____ Date: _____

M   T   W   Th   F

Mute Dancers: How to Watch a Hummingbird / The Hummingbird That Lived Through Winter, p. 408

Vocabulary & Spelling Workshop: Context Clues, p. 423

Directed Reading
"Mute Dancers: How to Watch a Hummingbird"
- **Reading Level:** Moderate
- **Difficulty Consideration:** Vocabulary and sentence length
- **Ease Factor:** Subject matter

"The Hummingbird That Lived Through Winter"
- **Reading Level:** Moderate
- **Difficulty Consideration:** Prior knowledge needed
- **Ease Factor:** Length

Pacing
- **Regular Schedule:** 3 days
- **Block Schedule:** 1.5 days

Objectives
Studying this lesson will enable students to
- compare literary selections of different genres on the same topic
- use reading skills such as setting a purpose for reading
- define description and compare its effects in these selections
- describe literary accomplishments of Diane Ackerman and William Saroyan
- compare the ways people respond to nature

Before Reading

Preview and Motivate
Choose from the following materials to preview the lesson and motivate your students:
____   Before Reading, *SE/ATE*, p. 408
____   Build Background, Set Purpose, and Practice Vocabulary, *Meeting the Standards Unit 4*, p. 36

During Reading

Teach the Selection(s)
Choose from the following resources to teach the selection(s):
____   During Reading, *SE/ATE*, pp. 409–413
____   Grammar Skills: Compound Words, *ATE*, p. 411
____   Speaking & Listening Skills: Group Discussion Etiquette, *ATE*, p. 413
____   Analyze Literature: Sensory Details, *Meeting the Standards Unit 4*, p. 37

Differentiate Instruction
Consider the following alternative teaching options to differentiate instruction:
____   English Language Learning, *ATE*, pp. 410, 412
____   Enrichment, *ATE*, p. 410
____   Reading Strategies and Skills Practice: Set Purpose, *Differentiated Instruction for Developing Readers*, pp. 28–30

After Reading

Review and Extend

Use the following materials to review and extend the lesson:

____ After Reading, *SE/ATE*, pp. 411, 414

____ Analyze Literature: Sensory Details (continued), *Meeting the Standards Unit 4*, p. 38

____ Analyze Literature: Essay and Fiction, *Meeting the Standards Unit 4*, p. 39

____ Using Reading Strategies: Make Connections, *Meeting the Standards Unit 4*, p. 40

____ What Do You Think? *Meeting the Standards Unit 4*, p. 45

____ Lifelong Learning: Research Myths and Legends, *Exceeding the Standards: Extension Activities*, p. 11

____ Predicate Nouns, Pronouns, and Adjectives, *Exceeding the Standards: Grammar & Style*, pp. 88–91

Teach the Workshop(s)

Select from the following materials to teach the workshop(s):

____ Vocabulary & Spelling: Context Clues, *SE/ATE*, p. 423

____ Language Arts Handbook Section 2.1, Using Context Clues, *SE/ATE*, p. 836

____ Context Clues, *Exceeding the Standards: Vocabulary & Spelling*, pp. 35–36

____ Using Context Clues I: Comparison and Contrast, *Exceeding the Standards: Vocabulary & Spelling*, pp. 37–38

____ Using Context Clues II: Restatement and Apposition, *Exceeding the Standards: Vocabulary & Spelling*, pp. 39–40

____ Using Context Clues III: Examples and Cause and Effect, *Exceeding the Standards: Vocabulary & Spelling*, pp. 41–42

Assess

Administer the following assessment tool(s):

____ Selection Quiz: Focus on "Mute Dancers: How to Watch a Hummingbird," *Meeting the Standards Unit 4*, pp. 41–42

____ Selection Quiz: Focus on "The Hummingbird That Lived Through Winter," *Meeting the Standards Unit 4*, pp. 43–44

____ Lesson Test, *Assessment Guide*, pp. 124–126

Technology Tools

Enhance the lesson with interactive activities offered in these technology supplements:

- EMC Launchpad
- Annotated Teacher's Edition on CD
- Interactive Student Text on CD
- Exam*View*® Assessment Suite on CD
- Visual Teaching Package
- ETS Online Criterion-Based Essay Grader (Grades 9–12)
- EMC Audio Library
- EMC E-Library
- **mirrorsandwindows.com**

Name: _____ Date: _____

M   T   W   Th   F

The Face of the Deep is Frozen / Fire and Ice, p. 415

Directed Reading
- **Reading Level:** Challenging
- **Difficulty Consideration:** Concepts and vocabulary
- **Ease Factor:** Gripping content

Pacing
- **Regular Schedule:** 3 days
- **Block Schedule:** 1.5 days

Objectives
Studying this lesson will enable students to
- use reading skills such as context clues
- define description and recognize its role in the selection
- describe how Jennifer Armstrong develops her stories
- appreciate a story about testing limits in a harsh environment

Before Reading

Preview and Motivate
Choose from the following materials to preview the lesson and motivate your students:
_____ Before Reading, *SE/ATE*, p. 415
_____ Creative Writing: Expedition Want Ad, *Meeting the Standards Unit 4*, pp. 46–47

During Reading

Teach the Selection(s)
Choose from the following resources to teach the selection(s):
_____ During Reading, *SE/ATE*, pp. 416–420
_____ Literature Connection: "Fire and Ice," *SE/ATE*, p. 421
_____ Vocabulary Skills: Jargon, *ATE*, p. 417
_____ Grammar Skills: Capitalization Rules, *ATE*, p. 419
_____ Speaking & Listening Skills: Person-to-Person Conversation, *ATE*, p. 421
_____ Analyze Literature: Rhyme Scheme, *Meeting the Standards Unit 4*, p. 48

Differentiate Instruction
Consider the following alternative teaching options to differentiate instruction:
_____ English Language Learning, *ATE*, p. 418
_____ Enrichment, *ATE*, p. 420

After Reading

Review and Extend
Use the following materials to review and extend the lesson:
_____ After Reading, *SE/ATE*, pp. 420, 422
_____ Analyze Literature: Make Judgments, *Meeting the Standards Unit 4*, p. 49
_____ Expository Writing: Compare-and-Contrast Essay, *Meeting the Standards Unit 4*, p. 50
_____ Use Reading Strategies: Visualize with a Storyboard, *Meeting the Standards Unit 4*, p. 51
_____ Critical Literacy: Hold a Debate, *Exceeding the Standards: Extension Activities*, pp. 12–13

Assess

Administer the following assessment tool(s):

_____ Selection Quiz, *Meeting the Standards Unit 4*, p. 52

_____ Lesson Test, *Assessment Guide*, pp. 127–129

Technology Tools

Enhance the lesson with interactive activities offered in these technology supplements:

- EMC Launchpad
- Annotated Teacher's Edition on CD
- Interactive Student Text on CD
- Exam *View*® Assessment Suite on CD
- Visual Teaching Package
- ETS Online Criterion-Based Essay Grader (Grades 9–12)
- EMC Audio Library
- EMC E-Library
- **mirrorsandwindows.com**

Name: _____ Date: _____

M T W Th F

Hmong Storycloth / An Unforgettable Journey, p. 424

Directed Reading	**Objectives**
• **Reading Level:** Moderate	Studying this lesson will enable students to
• **Difficulty Consideration:** Topic	• use reading skills such as identifying a
• **Ease Factor:** Visual format and point	sequence of events
of view	• evaluate author's purpose in visual media
	such as a storycloth
Pacing	• compare visual and written narratives by
• **Regular Schedule:** 3 days	two Loatian refugees
• **Block Schedule:** 1.5 days	• appreciate true stories of emigration

Before Reading

Preview and Motivate

Choose from the following materials to preview the lesson and motivate your students:

_____ Before Reading, *SE/ATE*, p. 424

_____ Build Background: Hmong Profile, *Meeting the Standards Unit 4*, p. 53

_____ Build Background: Immigration Storycloth, *Meeting the Standards Unit 4*, p. 54

During Reading

Teach the Selection(s)

Choose from the following resources to teach the selection(s):

_____ During Reading, *SE/ATE*, p. 425

_____ Primary Source Connection: "An Unforgettable Journey," *SE/ATE*, pp. 426–430

_____ Grammar Skills: Dependent and Independent Clauses, *ATE*, p. 427

_____ Grammar Skills: Direct Quotations, *ATE*, p. 429

_____ Text-to-Text Connection, *Meeting the Standards Unit 4*, p. 55

_____ Expository and Creative Writing: Point of View, *Meeting the Standards Unit 4*, p. 56

Differentiate Instruction

Consider the following alternative teaching options to differentiate instruction:

_____ Enrichment, *ATE*, pp. 428, 430

_____ Reading Strategies and Skills Practice: Take Notes, *Differentiated Instruction for Developing Readers*, pp. 31–33

After Reading

Review and Extend

Use the following materials to review and extend the lesson:

_____ After Reading, *SE/ATE*, pp. 425, 431

_____ Creative Writing: Culture Shock, *Meeting the Standards Unit 4*, p. 57

Assess

Administer the following assessment tool(s):

_____ Selection Quiz, *Meeting the Standards Unit 4*, p. 58

_____ Lesson Test, *Assessment Guide*, pp. 130–132

Technology Tools

Enhance the lesson with interactive activities offered in these technology supplements:

- EMC Launchpad
- Annotated Teacher's Edition on CD
- Interactive Student Text on CD
- Exam*View*® Assessment Suite on CD
- Visual Teaching Package
- ETS Online Criterion-Based Essay Grader (Grades 9–12)
- EMC Audio Library
- EMC E-Library
- **mirrorsandwindows.com**

Name: _____ Date: _____

M   T   W   Th   F

Dust Bowl Photographs / Dust Changes America, p. 432

Directed Reading
- **Reading Level:** Moderate
- **Difficulty Consideration:** Topic
- **Ease Factor:** Visual format and imagery

Pacing
- **Regular Schedule:** 2 days
- **Block Schedule:** 1 day

Objectives
Studying this lesson will enable students to
- use reading skills such as activating prior knowledge
- practice determining the purpose of visual media
- describe the work of Arthur Rothstein and Margaret Bourke-White
- appreciate the historical value of photographs

Before Reading

Preview and Motivate
Choose from the following materials to preview the lesson and motivate your students:
_____   Before Reading, *SE/ATE*, p. 432
_____   Build Background: Woody Guthrie Song, *Meeting the Standards Unit 4*, p. 59

During Reading

Teach the Selection(s)
Choose from the following resources to teach the selection(s):
_____   During Reading, *SE/ATE*, pp. 433–435
_____   Informational Text Connection: "Dust Changes America," *SE/ATE*, pp. 436–438
_____   History Connection: The New Deal, *SE/ATE*, p. 438
_____   Speaking & Listening Skills: Oral Summary, *ATE*, p. 435
_____   Reading Skills: Draw Conclusions, *ATE*, p. 437
_____   Text-to-Text Connection: Dust Bowl Exhibit, *Meeting the Standards Unit 4*, p. 60
_____   Use Reading Strategies: Make an Outline, *Meeting the Standards Unit 4*, pp. 61–62

Differentiate Instruction
Consider the following alternative teaching options to differentiate instruction:
_____   Visual Learning, *ATE*, pp. 434, 436
_____   Enrichment, *ATE*, p. 434
_____   Critical Viewing Activity: Documentary Photography, *Differentiated Instruction for Advanced Students*, p. 23
_____   Reading Strategies and Skills Practice: Take Notes, *Differentiated Instruction for Developing Readers*, pp. 31–33

After Reading

Review and Extend

Use the following materials to review and extend the lesson:

____ After Reading, *SE/ATE*, pp. 435, 439
____ Applied Writing: Photojournalism in a Natural Disaster, *Meeting the Standards Unit 4*, p. 63
____ Expository Writing: Explain Using Cause and Effect, *Exceeding the Standards: Writing*, pp. 23–30

Assess

Administer the following assessment tool(s):

____ Selection Quiz, *Meeting the Standards Unit 4*, pp. 64–65
____ Lesson Test, *Assessment Guide*, pp. 133–135

Technology Tools

Enhance the lesson with interactive activities offered in these technology supplements:

- EMC Launchpad
- Annotated Teacher's Edition on CD
- Interactive Student Text on CD
- Exam*View*® Assessment Suite on CD
- Visual Teaching Package
- ETS Online Criterion-Based Essay Grader (Grades 9–12)
- EMC Audio Library
- EMC E-Library
- **mirrorsandwindows.com**

Name: _____ Date: _____

M   T   W   Th   F

Death in the Open, p. 440

Independent Reading
- **Reading Level:** Challenging
- **Difficulty Consideration:** Concepts and vocabulary
- **Ease Factor:** Imagery

Pacing
- **Regular Schedule:** 1 day
- **Block Schedule:** 0.5 day

Objectives
Studying this lesson will enable students to
- read with developing fluency
- read silently with comprehension for a sustained period of time

Before Reading

Preview and Motivate
Choose from the following materials to preview the lesson and motivate your students:
_____ Before Reading, *SE/ATE*, p. 440
_____ Practice Vocabulary, *Meeting the Standards Unit 4*, p. 66

During Reading

Teach the Selection(s)
Choose from the following resources to teach the selection(s):
_____ During Reading, *SE/ATE*, pp. 440–442
_____ Reading Skills: Identify the Main Idea, *ATE*, p. 442
_____ Analyze Literature: Diction, *Meeting the Standards Unit 4*, p. 67

Differentiate Instruction
Consider the following alternative teaching options to differentiate instruction:
_____ Author's Purpose Analysis: Evaluate Effectiveness, *Differentiated Instruction for Advanced Readers*, p. 24

After Reading

Review and Extend
Use the following materials to review and extend the lesson:
_____ After Reading, *SE/ATE*, p. 442
_____ Use Reading Skills: Identify Main Idea, *Meeting the Standards Unit 4*, p. 68
_____ Describe and Critique: Informational Text, *Meeting the Standards Unit 4*, pp. 70–73

Assess
Administer the following assessment tool(s):
_____ Selection Quiz, *Meeting the Standards Unit 4*, p. 69
_____ Lesson Test, *Assessment Guide*, pp. 136–138

Technology Tools

Enhance the lesson with interactive activities offered in these technology supplements:

- EMC Launchpad
- Annotated Teacher's Edition on CD
- Interactive Student Text on CD
- Exam*View*® Assessment Suite on CD
- Visual Teaching Package
- ETS Online Criterion-Based Essay Grader (Grades 9–12)
- EMC Audio Library
- EMC E-Library
- **mirrorsandwindows.com**

Name: _____ Date: _____

M   T   W   Th   F

Astonishing Animals, p. 443

Independent Reading
- **Reading Level:** Easy
- **Difficulty Consideration:** Vocabulary
- **Ease Factor:** Visual format and imagery

Pacing
- **Regular Schedule:** 1 day
- **Block Schedule:** 0.5 day

Objectives
Studying this lesson will enable students to
- read with developing fluency
- read silently with comprehension for a sustained period of time
- interpret visual media

Before Reading

Preview and Motivate
Choose from the following materials to preview the lesson and motivate your students:
_____   Before Reading, *SE/ATE*, p. 443
_____   Practice Vocabulary, *Meeting the Standards Unit 4*, pp. 74–75
_____   Set Purpose, *Meeting the Standards Unit 4*, p. 76

During Reading

Teach the Selection(s)
Choose from the following resources to teach the selection(s):
_____   During Reading, *SE/ATE*, pp. 443–445
_____   Vocabulary Skills: Compound Words, *ATE*, p. 445
_____   Analyze Literature: Compare and Contrast, *Meeting the Standards Unit 4*, p. 77

Differentiate Instruction
Consider the following alternative teaching options to differentiate instruction:
_____   Enrichment, *ATE*, p. 446
_____   Visual Media Project: Art Gallery, *Differentiated Instruction for Advanced Readers*, pp. 25–26

After Reading

Review and Extend
Use the following materials to review and extend the lesson:
_____   After Reading, *SE/ATE*, p. 446
_____   Notes for Journal Entry, *Meeting the Standards Unit 4*, p. 78
_____   Describe and Critique: Visual Media, *Meeting the Standards Unit 4*, pp. 79–82

Assess
Administer the following assessment tool(s):
_____   Lesson Test, *Assessment Guide*, pp. 139–141

Technology Tools

Enhance the lesson with interactive activities offered in these technology supplements:

- EMC Launchpad
- Annotated Teacher's Edition on CD
- Interactive Student Text on CD
- Exam*View*® Assessment Suite on CD
- Visual Teaching Package
- ETS Online Criterion-Based Essay Grader (Grades 9–12)
- EMC Audio Library
- EMC E-Library
- **mirrorsandwindows.com**

Name: _____ Date: _____
M   T   W   Th   F

Writing Workshop: Descriptive Writing—Descriptive Essay, p. 448

Pacing
- **Regular Schedule:** 3 days
- **Block Schedule:** 1.5 days

Objectives
Participating in this lesson will help enable students to
- write a descriptive essay that conveys a personal impression in its introduction
- write a descriptive essay that has a clear organizational pattern
- write a descriptive essay that uses figurative language and sensory details, as well as strong verbs and active voice
- write a descriptive essay that includes appropriate personal thoughts and feelings
- write a descriptive essay that has a conclusion that summarizes and conveys a new insight

Teach the Workshop
Select from the following resources to teach the workshop:
_____ Descriptive Writing: Descriptive Essay, *SE/ATE*, pp. 448–453
_____ Writing Skills: Similes and Metaphors, *ATE*, p. 449
_____ Writing Skills: Revise, *ATE*, p. 451
_____ Writing Skills: Review and Reflect on the Writing Process, *ATE*, p. 453
_____ Language Arts Handbook Section 4.1, The Writing Process, *SE/ATE*, pp. 888–897
_____ Language Arts Handbook Section 4.2, Modes and Purposes of Writing, *SE/ATE*, p. 897

Differentiate Instruction
Consider the following alternative teaching options to differentiate instruction:
_____ Reading Proficiency and Visual Learning, *ATE*, p. 450
_____ English Language Learning, *ATE*, p. 450
_____ Enrichment, *ATE*, p. 452
_____ Reading Proficiency, p. 452

Review and Extend
Use the following materials to review and extend the lesson:
_____ Descriptive Writing: Create an Analogy, *Exceeding the Standards: Writing*, pp. 31–38

Technology Tools
Enhance the lesson with interactive activities offered in these technology supplements:
- EMC Launchpad
- Annotated Teacher's Edition on CD
- Interactive Student Text on CD
- Exam*View*® Assessment Suite on CD
- Visual Teaching Package
- ETS Online Criterion-Based Essay Grader (Grades 9–12)
- EMC Audio Library
- EMC E-Library
- **mirrorsandwindows.com**

LESSON PLAN

Viewing Workshop: Critical Viewing, p. 454

Pacing
- **Regular Schedule:** 2 days
- **Block Schedule:** 1 day

Objectives
Participating in this lesson will help enable students to
- plan and deliver a visual presentation that effectively employs visuals to enhance appeal
- plan and deliver a clear and well-organized visual presentation
- plan a visual presentation that supports main ideas with evidence
- deliver a visual presentation that exhibits appropriate volume and pacing and effective nonverbal expression
- respond helpfully to audience questions

Teach the Workshop
Select from the following resources to teach the workshop:
____ Viewing Workshop: Critical Viewing, *SE/ATE*, pp. 454–455
____ Speaking & Listening Skills: Audience Questions, *ATE*, p. 455
____ Language Arts Handbook Section 7.1, Verbal and Nonverbal Communication, *SE/ATE*, p. 912
____ Language Arts Handbook Section 7.4, Asking and Answer Questions, *SE/ATE*, p. 915
____ Language Arts Handbook Section 7.6, Public Speaking, *SE/ATE*, pp. 916–917
____ Language Arts Handbook Section 7.10, Preparing a Multimedia Presentation, *SE/ATE*, p. 920

Differentiate Instruction
Consider the following alternative teaching options to differentiate instruction:
____ Auditory Learning, *ATE*, p. 454

Review and Extend
Use the following materials to review and extend the lesson:
____ Critical Viewing, *Exceeding the Standards: Speaking & Listening*, pp. 10–12

Technology Tools
Enhance the lesson with interactive activities offered in these technology supplements:
- EMC Launchpad
- Annotated Teacher's Edition on CD
- Interactive Student Text on CD
- Exam*View*® Assessment Suite on CD
- Visual Teaching Package
- ETS Online Criterion-Based Essay Grader (Grades 9–12)
- EMC Audio Library
- EMC E-Library
- **mirrorsandwindows.com**

Name: _____ Date: _____

M   T   W   Th   F

Test Practice Workshop, p. 456

Pacing
- **Regular Schedule:** 1 day
- **Block Schedule:** 0.5 day

Objectives
Participating in this lesson will help enable students to
- write a descriptive essay based on a timed writing prompt

- answer standardized test questions that demonstrate revising and editing skills
- demonstrate the ability to make inferences from a reading by answering standardized questions

Teach the Workshop
Select from the following resources to teach the workshop:
_____ Writing Skills: Descriptive Essay, *SE/ATE*, p. 456
_____ Revising and Editing Skills, *SE/ATE*, p. 457
_____ Reading Skills, *SE/ATE*, pp. 458–459
_____ Test-Taking Skills: Eliminate Incorrect Responses, *ATE*, p. 459
_____ Language Arts Handbook Section 8.1, Preparing for Tests, *SE/ATE*, p. 921
_____ Language Arts Handbook Section 8.2, Strategies for Taking Standardized Tests, *SE/ATE*, pp. 921–922
_____ Language Arts Handbook Section 8.4, Answering Multiple-Choice Questions, *SE/ATE*, p. 922
_____ Language Arts Handbook Section 8.5, Answering Reading Comprehension Questions, *SE/ATE*, p. 923
_____ Test-Taking Skills and Strategies, *Exceeding the Standards: Test Practice*, pp. 1–4

Differentiate Instruction
Consider the following alternative teaching options to differentiate instruction:
_____ English Language Learning, *ATE*, p. 458

Review and Extend
Use the following materials to review and extend the lesson:
_____ Nonfiction Study Guide: Practice Test, *Meeting the Standards Unit 4*, pp. 11–16
_____ Descriptive Essay Practice Test: Reading, *Exceeding the Standards: Test Practice*, pp. 10–12

Technology Tools
Enhance the lesson with interactive activities offered in these technology supplements:
- EMC Launchpad
- Annotated Teacher's Edition on CD
- Interactive Student Text on CD
- Exam*View*® Assessment Suite on CD
- Visual Teaching Package
- ETS Online Criterion-Based Essay Grader (Grades 9–12)
- EMC Audio Library
- EMC E-Library
- **mirrorsandwindows.com**

LESSON PLAN

Name: _____ Date: _____

Unit 5 Poetry Opener, p. 460

Pacing	Objectives
• **Regular Schedule:** 1 day • **Block Schedule:** 0.5 day	Studying this lesson will enable students to • connect a theme expressed in a poem to their own lives and to the world around them • understand different elements and forms of poetry

Plan the Unit

Use the following resources to plan instruction for this unit:

____ Unit 5 Visual Planning Guide: Unit-Based Resources, *ATE*, pp. 460A–460B

____ Unit 5 Visual Planning Guide: Lesson-by-Lesson Resources, *ATE*, pp. 460C–460F

____ Unit 5 Scope & Sequence Guide, *ATE*, pp. 460E–460J

____ Unit 5 Building Vocabulary, *ATE*, pp. 460K–460L

____ Launch the Unit, *ATE*, p. 460

Teach the Unit Opener

Choose from the following resources to teach the unit opener:

____ Unit 5 Overview, *SE/ATE*, pp. 460–461

____ Introduction to Poetry, *SE/ATE*, pp. 462–463

____ Poetry Study Guide: Introduction to Poetry and Applying Introduction to Poetry to the Selections, *Meeting the Standards Unit 5*, pp. 1–4

____ Poetry Study Guide: Master Vocabulary List, *Meeting the Standards Unit 5*, p. 17

Extend the Unit

Choose from the following resources to extend the unit:

____ For Your Reading List, *SE/ATE*, p. 523

____ Unit 5, *Exceeding the Standards: Grammar & Style*, pp. 113–131

____ Deliver an Oral Interpretation of a Poem, *Exceeding the Standards: Literature & Reading*, pp. 11–13

____ Lifelong Learning: Making Good Choices: Part 1, *Exceeding the Standards: Special Topics*, pp. 18–19

____ Career Skills Development: Analyzing Your Skills and Values, *Exceeding the Standards: Special Topics*, pp. 20–21

____ Unit 5, *Exceeding the Standards: Vocabulary & Spelling*, pp. 47–57

Assess

Administer the following assessment tool(s):

____ Formative Surveys 1 and 2, *Assessment Guide*, pp. 3–20

____ Reading Fluency Assessments, Passages 1 and 2, *Assessment Guide*, pp. 301–302

____ Unit 5 Exam, *Assessment Guide*, pp. 269–272

Technology Tools

Enhance the lesson with interactive activities offered in these technology supplements:

- EMC Launchpad
- Annotated Teacher's Edition on CD
- Interactive Student Text on CD
- Exam*View*® Assessment Suite on CD
- Visual Teaching Package
- ETS Online Criterion-Based Essay Grader (Grades 9–12)
- EMC Audio Library
- EMC E-Library
- **mirrorsandwindows.com**

Name: _____ Date: _____

Literary Element: Understanding Imagery and Figurative Language, p. 464

Gold, p. 466

Guided Reading: Reading Model
- **Reading Level:** Easy
- **Difficulty Consideration:** None
- **Ease Factor:** Imagery and straightforward language

Pacing
- **Regular Schedule:** 1 day
- **Block Schedule:** 0.5 day

Objectives

Studying this lesson will enable students to
- use reading skills such as identifying the main idea
- define imagery and recognize how it is used in the poem
- define the literary accomplishments of Pat Mora and explain how home and nature influence her writing
- appreciate a lyric poem that celebrates feeling at home

Before Reading

Teach the Feature(s)

Select from the following resources to teach the feature(s):

_____   Literary Element: Understanding Imagery and Figurative Language, *SE/ATE*, p. 464
_____   Differentiated Instruction: English Language Learning, *ATE*, p. 464
_____   Differentiated Instruction: Reading Proficiency, *ATE*, p. 464
_____   Nonfiction Study Guide: Understanding Imagery and Figurative Language and Applying Imagery and Figurative Language to the Selections, *Meeting the Standards Unit 5*, pp. 5–7

Preview and Motivate

Choose from the following materials to preview the lesson and motivate your students:

_____   Poetry Reading Model, *SE/ATE*, p. 465
_____   Before Reading, *SE/ATE*, p. 466
_____   How to Read Poetry, *Meeting the Standards Unit 5*, pp. 19–20
_____   Build Background: A Place of Your Own, *Meeting the Standards Unit 5*, pp. 21–22

During Reading

Teach the Selection(s)

Choose from the following resources to teach the selection(s):

_____   During Reading, *SE/ATE*, p. 467
_____   Vocabulary: Creating a Regional Lexicon, *Meeting the Standards Unit 5*, pp. 23–24

After Reading

Review and Extend

Use the following materials to review and extend the lesson:

_____   After Reading, *SE/ATE*, p. 468
_____   Creative Writing: Adapting a Regional Poem, *Meeting the Standards Unit 5*, p. 25

Assess

Administer the following assessment tool(s):

____ Selection Quiz, *Meeting the Standards Unit 5,* p. 26

____ Lesson Test, *Assessment Guide,* pp. 142–143

Technology Tools

Enhance the lesson with interactive activities offered in these technology supplements:

- *⌀* EMC Launchpad
- ⊕ Annotated Teacher's Edition on CD
- ⊕ Interactive Student Text on CD
- ⊕ Exam*View*® Assessment Suite on CD
- ▦ Visual Teaching Package
- *⌀* ETS Online Criterion-Based Essay Grader (Grades 9–12)
- ⌒ EMC Audio Library
- *⌀* EMC E-Library
- *⌀* **mirrorsandwindows.com**

Name: _____ Date: _____

M   T   W   Th   F

Feel Like a Bird, p. 469

Guided Reading: Reading Model	Objectives
• **Reading Level:** Moderate	Studying this lesson will enable students to
• **Difficulty Consideration:** Punctuation, capitalization, and diction	• use reading skills such as monitor comprehension
• **Ease Factor:** Length	• define metaphor and simile and recognize how the poet uses them
Pacing	• describe how the natural world influenced May Swenson's writing
• **Regular Schedule:** 2 days	• appreciate a playful poem that closely observes and celebrates birds
• **Block Schedule:** 1 day	

Before Reading

Preview and Motivate

Choose from the following materials to preview the lesson and motivate your students:

_____   Poetry Reading Model, *SE/ATE*, p. 465

_____   Before Reading, *SE/ATE*, p. 469

_____   Analyze Literature: Previewing Metaphors and Similes, *Meeting the Standards Unit 5*, p. 27

During Reading

Teach the Selection(s)

Choose from the following resources to teach the selection(s):

_____   During Reading, *SE/ATE*, pp. 470–471

_____   Use Reading Skills: Monitor Comprehension, *Meeting the Standards Unit 5*, p. 28

Differentiate Instruction

Consider the following alternative teaching options to differentiate instruction:

_____   Enrichment, *ATE*, p. 471

_____   English Language Learning, *ATE*, p. 471

_____   Reading Strategies and Skills Practice: Set Purpose, *Differentiated Instruction for Developing Readers*, pp. 34–36

After Reading

Review and Extend

Use the following materials to review and extend the lesson:

_____   After Reading, *SE/ATE*, p. 472

_____   Use Reading Strategies: Make Connections, *Meeting the Standards Unit 5*, p. 29

Assess

Administer the following assessment tool(s):

_____   Selection Quiz, *Meeting the Standards Unit 5*, p. 30

_____   Lesson Test, *Assessment Guide*, pp. 144–145

Technology Tools

Enhance the lesson with interactive activities offered in these technology supplements:

- EMC Launchpad
- Annotated Teacher's Edition on CD
- Interactive Student Text on CD
- Exam*View*® Assessment Suite on CD
- Visual Teaching Package
- ETS Online Criterion-Based Essay Grader (Grades 9–12)
- EMC Audio Library
- EMC E-Library
- **mirrorsandwindows.com**

Name: _____ Date: _____

Literary Element: Understanding Sound Devices, p. 473

Father William, p. 475

Grammar & Style Workshop: Personal and Possessive Pronouns, p. 480

Guided Reading: Reading Model
- **Reading Level:** Easy
- **Difficulty Consideration:** Vocabulary
- **Ease Factor:** Rhythm and humor

Pacing
- **Regular Schedule:** 2 days
- **Block Schedule:** 1 day

Objectives

Studying this lesson will enable students to
- use reading skills such as analyzing the effects of form on meaning
- define rhyme and recognize its effect on tone
- define the literary accomplishments of Lewis Carroll
- appreciate a humorous poem

Before Reading

Teach the Feature(s)

Select from the following resources to teach the feature(s):

_____ Literary Element: Understanding Sound Devices, *SE/ATE*, p. 473

_____ Differentiated Instruction: Enrichment, *ATE*, p. 474

_____ Poetry Study Guide: Understanding Sound Devices and Applying Sound Devices to the Selections, *Meeting the Standards Unit 5*, pp. 8–10

Preview and Motivate

Choose from the following materials to preview the lesson and motivate your students:

_____ Poetry Reading Model, *SE/ATE*, p. 465

_____ Before Reading, *SE/ATE*, p. 475

_____ Vocabulary: Prefixes and Suffixes, *Meeting the Standards Unit 5*, pp. 31–32

During Reading

Teach the Selection(s)

Choose from the following resources to teach the selection(s):

_____ During Reading, *SE/ATE*, pp. 476–478

_____ Cultural Connection: Wonderland, *SE/ATE*, p. 478

_____ Grammar Skills: Exclamation Marks, *ATE*, p. 477

_____ Analyze Literature: Rhyme, *Meeting the Standards Unit 5*, pp. 33–34

Differentiate Instruction

Consider the following alternative teaching options to differentiate instruction:

_____ Enrichment, *ATE*, p. 478

_____ Analyze Text Organization, *Differentiated Instruction for English Language Learners*, pp. 132–138

_____ Author Study: The Word of Lewis Carroll, *Differentiated Instruction for Advanced Students*, pp. 27–28

After Reading

Review and Extend

Use the following materials to review and extend the lesson:

_____   After Reading, *SE/ATE*, p. 479
_____   Analyze Literature: Parody, *Meeting the Standards Unit 5*, p. 35

Teach the Workshop(s)

Select from the following materials to teach the workshop(s):

_____   Grammar & Style: Personal and Possessive Pronouns, *SE/ATE*, p. 480
_____   Language Arts Handbook Section 3.4, Pronouns, *SE/ATE*, pp. 856–858
_____   Pronouns, *Exceeding the Standards: Grammar & Style*, pp. 33–36
_____   Pronouns and Antecedents, *Exceeding the Standards: Grammar & Style*, pp. 37–39
_____   Subject and Object Pronouns, *Exceeding the Standards: Grammar & Style*, pp. 40–42
_____   Possessive Pronouns, *Exceeding the Standards: Grammar & Style*, pp. 43–45

Assess

Administer the following assessment tool(s):

_____   Selection Quiz, *Meeting the Standards Unit 5*, p. 36
_____   Lesson Test, *Assessment Guide*, pp. 146–147

Technology Tools

Enhance the lesson with interactive activities offered in these technology supplements:

- EMC Launchpad
- Annotated Teacher's Edition on CD
- Interactive Student Text on CD
- Exam*View*® Assessment Suite on CD
- Visual Teaching Package
- ETS Online Criterion-Based Essay Grader (Grades 9–12)
- EMC Audio Library
- EMC E-Library
- **mirrorsandwindows.com**

Name: _____ Date: _____
M   T   W   Th   F

Blackberry Eating, p. 481

Vocabulary & Spelling Workshop: Synonyms and Antonyms, p. 484

Guided Reading: Reading Model
- **Reading Level:** Moderate
- **Difficulty Consideration:** Vocabulary and alliteration
- **Ease Factor:** Sensory details

Pacing
- **Regular Schedule:** 1 day
- **Block Schedule:** 0.5 day

Objectives
Studying this lesson will enable students to
- use reading skills such as identifying the author's perspective
- recognize alliteration
- explain how a poem connects the self and the world
- appreciate a poem inspired by an enjoyable experience

Before Reading

Preview and Motivate

Choose from the following materials to preview the lesson and motivate your students:

____ Poetry Reading Model, *SE/ATE*, p. 465

____ Before Reading, *SE/ATE*, p. 481

____ Build Background: Appreciating Life, *Meeting the Standards Unit 5*, p. 37

____ Creative Writing: Poem with Imagery, *Meeting the Standards Unit 5*, p. 38

During Reading

Teach the Selection(s)

Choose from the following resources to teach the selection(s):

____ During Reading, *SE/ATE*, p. 482

____ Analyze Literature: Expository Writing, *Meeting the Standards Unit 5*, p. 39

Differentiate Instruction

Consider the following alternative teaching options to differentiate instruction:

____ Reading Strategies and Skills: Visualize, *Differentiated Instruction for Developing Readers*, pp. 37–39

After Reading

Review and Extend

Use the following materials to review and extend the lesson:

____ After Reading, *SE/ATE*, p. 483

____ Literary Element: Understanding Sound Devices, *SE/ATE*, p. 473

____ Text-to-Text Connection, *Meeting the Standards Unit 5*, p. 40

Teach the Workshop(s)

Select from the following materials to teach the workshop(s):

____ Vocabulary & Spelling: Synonyms and Antonyms, *SE/ATE*, p. 484

____ Language Arts Handbook Section 2.3, Using a Dictionary, *SE/ATE*, p. 841

____ Synonyms and Antonyms, *Exceeding the Standards: Vocabulary & Spelling*, pp. 68–69

Assess

Administer the following assessment tool(s):

____ Selection Quiz, *Meeting the Standards Unit 5*, p. 41

____ Lesson Test, *Assessment Guide*, pp. 148–149

Technology Tools

Enhance the lesson with interactive activities offered in these technology supplements:

- EMC Launchpad
- Annotated Teacher's Edition on CD
- Interactive Student Text on CD
- Exam*View*® Assessment Suite on CD
- Visual Teaching Package
- ETS Online Criterion-Based Essay Grader (Grades 9–12)
- EMC Audio Library
- EMC E-Library
- **mirrorsandwindows.com**

LESSON PLAN

Name: _____ Date: _____

M   T   W   Th   F

The Village Blacksmith, p. 485

Grammar & Style Workshop: Nouns: Proper, Plural, Possessive, and Collective, p. 490

Directed Reading
- **Reading Level:** Moderate
- **Difficulty Consideration:** Length and archaic vocabulary
- **Ease Factor:** Rhythm and rhyme

Pacing
- **Regular Schedule:** 2 days
- **Block Schedule:** 1 day

Objectives
Studying this lesson will enable students to
- use reading skills such as looking for context clues
- define and observe rhythm
- recognize Henry Wadsworth Longfellow and appreciate an iconic figure of early American life

---

Before Reading

Preview and Motivate

Choose from the following materials to preview the lesson and motivate your students:

____ Before Reading, *SE/ATE*, p. 485

____ Use Reading Skills: Evaluate Author's Purpose, *Meeting the Standards Unit 5*, pp. 42–43

During Reading

Teach the Selection(s)

Choose from the following resources to teach the selection(s):

____ During Reading, *SE/ATE*, pp. 486–488

____ Writing Skills: Alliteration, *ATE*, p. 487

____ Art Connection: A Currier and Ives Painting, *Meeting the Standards Unit 5*, p. 44

____ Vocabulary: Figurative Language, *Meeting the Standards Unit 5*, p. 45

Differentiate Instruction

Consider the following alternative teaching options to differentiate instruction:

____ English Language Learning, *ATE*, p. 488

After Reading

Review and Extend

Use the following materials to review and extend the lesson:

____ After Reading, *SE/ATE*, p. 489

____ Literary Element: Understanding Sound Devices, *SE/ATE*, p. 473

____ Media Literacy: Persuasive Speech, *Meeting the Standards Unit 5*, p. 46

Teach the Workshop(s)

Select from the following materials to teach the workshop(s):

_____ Grammar & Style: Nouns: Proper, Plural, Possessive, and Collective, *SE/ATE*, p. 490
_____ Language Arts Handbook Section 3.3, Nouns, *SE/ATE*, pp. 855–856
_____ Common and Proper Nouns, *Exceeding the Standards: Grammar & Style*, pp. 20–22
_____ Singular and Plural Nouns, *Exceeding the Standards: Grammar & Style*, pp. 23–24
_____ Possessive Nouns, *Exceeding the Standards: Grammar & Style*, pp. 25–27
_____ Compound Nouns and Collective Nouns, *Exceeding the Standards: Grammar & Style*, pp. 28–32

Assess

Administer the following assessment tool(s):

_____ Selection Quiz, *Meeting the Standards Unit 5*, p. 47
_____ Lesson Test, *Assessment Guide*, pp. 150–151

Technology Tools

Enhance the lesson with interactive activities offered in these technology supplements:

- EMC Launchpad
- Annotated Teacher's Edition on CD
- Interactive Student Text on CD
- Exam*View*® Assessment Suite on CD
- Visual Teaching Package

- ETS Online Criterion-Based Essay Grader (Grades 9–12)
- EMC Audio Library
- EMC E-Library
- **mirrorsandwindows.com**

LESSON PLAN

Name: _____ Date: _____

Mother to Son, p. 491

Directed Reading
- **Reading Level:** Easy
- **Difficulty Consideration:** Nonstandard English
- **Ease Factor:** Informal tone

Pacing
- **Regular Schedule:** 2 days
- **Block Schedule:** 1 day

Objectives
Studying this lesson will enable students to
- use reading skills such as identifying the main idea
- define repetition and recognize its effect in the selection
- describe Langston Hughes and explain the influence of the Harlem Renaissance on his writing
- contemplate a poem about appreciating life despite hard times

---

Before Reading

Preview and Motivate
Choose from the following materials to preview the lesson and motivate your students:
____   Before Reading, *SE/ATE*, p. 491
____   Collaborative Learning: History Research Project, *Meeting the Standards Unit 5*, p. 48
____   Applied Writing: Advice Column, *Meeting the Standards Unit 5*, p. 49

During Reading

Teach the Selection(s)
Choose from the following resources to teach the selection(s):
____   During Reading, *SE/ATE*, pp. 492–493
____   Analyze Literature: Effects of Form on Meaning, *Meeting the Standards Unit 5*, pp. 50–52
____   Literary Connection: Dialect, *Meeting the Standards Unit 5*, p. 53
____   Media Literacy: Listening to Recorded Interviews, *Meeting the Standards Unit 5*, p. 54

Differentiate Instruction
Consider the following alternative teaching options to differentiate instruction:
____   English Language Learning, *ATE*, p. 493
____   Reading Proficiency, *ATE*, p. 493
____   Cultural Context Project: The African-American Experience in the Twentieth Century, *Differentiated Instruction for Advanced Students*, pp. 29–30

After Reading

Review and Extend
Use the following materials to review and extend the lesson:
____   After Reading, *SE/ATE*, p. 494
____   Critical Literacy: Dramatic Reading, *Exceeding the Standards: Extension Activities*, p. 14
____   Interjections, *Exceeding the Standards: Grammar & Style*, pp. 126–128
____   Descriptive Writing: Create an Analogy, *Exceeding the Standards: Writing*, pp. 31–38

Assess

Administer the following assessment tool(s):

_____ Selection Quiz, *Meeting the Standards Unit 5,* p. 55

_____ Lesson Test, *Assessment Guide,* pp. 152–153

Technology Tools

Enhance the lesson with interactive activities offered in these technology supplements:

- EMC Launchpad
- Annotated Teacher's Edition on CD
- Interactive Student Text on CD
- Exam*View*® Assessment Suite on CD
- Visual Teaching Package
- ETS Online Criterion-Based Essay Grader (Grades 9–12)
- EMC Audio Library
- EMC E-Library
- **mirrorsandwindows.com**

LESSON PLAN

Name: _____ Date: _____

M   T   W   Th   F

Under the Apple Tree / *from* The Botany of Desire, p. 495

Grammar & Style Workshop: Reflexive and Intensive Pronouns, p. 501

Directed Reading
- **Reading Level:** Moderate
- **Difficulty Consideration:** Personification
- **Ease Factor:** Imagery

Pacing
- **Regular Schedule:** 2 days
- **Block Schedule:** 1 day

Objectives
Studying this lesson will enable students to
- use reading skills such as identifying multiple levels of meaning
- define free verse and recognize an example of this literary technique
- describe Diana Rivera's work and use writing by Michael Pollan to deepen understanding of her poetry
- appreciate a poem that expresses enjoyment in the close observation of nature

---

Before Reading

Preview and Motivate

Choose from the following materials to preview the lesson and motivate your students:

____   Before Reading, *SE/ATE*, p. 495
____   Build Background: A Special Place in Nature, *Meeting the Standards Unit 5*, p. 56
____   Literary Connection: The Legend of Johnny Appleseed, *Meeting the Standards Unit 5*, p. 57

During Reading

Teach the Selection(s)

Choose from the following resources to teach the selection(s):

____   During Reading, *SE/ATE*, pp. 496–497
____   Informational Text Connection: from *The Botany of Desire*, *SE/ATE*, pp. 498–499
____   Research Skills: Maps, *ATE*, p. 499
____   Analyze Literature: Figurative Language, *Meeting the Standards Unit 5*, pp. 58–59

Differentiate Instruction

Consider the following alternative teaching options to differentiate instruction:

____   Reading Proficiency, *ATE*, p. 497
____   English Language Learning, *ATE*, p. 497
____   Enrichment, *ATE*, p. 498

After Reading

Review and Extend

Use the following materials to review and extend the lesson:

____   After Reading, *SE/ATE*, pp. 497, 500
____   Introduction to Poetry: Elements of Poetry, *SE/ATE*, p. 463
____   Language Connection: Newly Coined Words, *Meeting the Standards Unit 5*, pp. 60–61
____   Expository Writing: A Comparison Paragraph, *Meeting the Standards Unit 5*, p. 62
____   Prepositions, *Exceeding the Standards: Grammar & Style*, pp. 116–119

Teach the Workshop(s)

Select from the following materials to teach the workshop(s):

_____ Grammar & Style: Reflexive and Intensive Pronouns, *SE/ATE*, p. 501

_____ Language Arts Handbook Section 3.4, Pronouns, *SE/ATE*, pp. 856–858

_____ Pronouns, *Exceeding the Standards: Grammar & Style*, pp. 33–36

Assess

Administer the following assessment tool(s):

_____ Selection Quiz, *Meeting the Standards Unit 5*, p. 63

_____ Lesson Test, *Assessment Guide*, pp. 154–156

Technology Tools

Enhance the lesson with interactive activities offered in these technology supplements:

- EMC Launchpad
- Annotated Teacher's Edition on CD
- Interactive Student Text on CD
- Exam*View*® Assessment Suite on CD
- Visual Teaching Package
- ETS Online Criterion-Based Essay Grader (Grades 9–12)
- EMC Audio Library
- EMC E-Library
- **mirrorsandwindows.com**

Name: _____   Date: _____
                                                                                    M   T   W   Th   F

The Tropics in New York, p. 502

Directed Reading
- **Reading Level:** Moderate
- **Difficulty Consideration:** Vocabulary and setting
- **Ease Factor:** Sensory details

Pacing
- **Regular Schedule:** 1 day
- **Block Schedule:** 0.5 day

Objectives
Studying this lesson will enable students to
- use reading skills such as analyzing cause and effect
- define rhyme scheme and recognize its effect in the selection
- describe literary accomplishments of Claude McKay and explain his part in the Harlem Renaissance
- analyze a poem about longing

Before Reading

Preview and Motivate
Choose from the following materials to preview the lesson and motivate your students:
_____   Before Reading, *SE/ATE*, p. 502
_____   Creative Writing: Memory Poem, *Meeting the Standards Unit 5*, p. 64
_____   Media Literacy: Do Research, *Meeting the Standards Unit 5*, p. 65

During Reading

Teach the Selection(s)
Choose from the following resources to teach the selection(s):
_____   During Reading, *SE/ATE*, p. 503
_____   Vocabulary: Homophones, *Meeting the Standards Unit 5*, p. 66
_____   Analyze Literature: Tying Mood to Meaning, *Meeting the Standards Unit 5*, p. 67

After Reading

Review and Extend
Use the following materials to review and extend the lesson:
_____   After Reading, *SE/ATE*, p. 504
_____   Applied Writing: An Editorial, *Meeting the Standards Unit 5*, p. 70
_____   Coordinating Conjunctions, *Exceeding the Standards: Grammar & Style*, pp. 120–122

Assess
Administer the following assessment tool(s):
_____   Selection Quiz, *Meeting the Standards Unit 5*, p. 71
_____   Lesson Test, *Assessment Guide*, pp. 157–158

Technology Tools

Enhance the lesson with interactive activities offered in these technology supplements:

- EMC Launchpad
- Annotated Teacher's Edition on CD
- Interactive Student Text on CD
- Exam*View*® Assessment Suite on CD
- Visual Teaching Package
- ETS Online Criterion-Based Essay Grader (Grades 9–12)
- EMC Audio Library
- EMC E-Library
- **mirrorsandwindows.com**

Name: _____ Date: _____

Unfolding Bud / How to Eat a Poem, p. 505

Directed Reading
"Unfolding Bud"
- **Reading Level:** Easy
- **Difficulty Consideration:** Metaphor
- **Ease Factor:** Vocabulary and length

"How to Eat a Poem"
- **Reading Level:** Moderate
- **Difficulty Consideration:** Poetic style
- **Ease Factor:** Simple, direct language

Pacing
- **Regular Schedule:** 2 days
- **Block Schedule:** 1 day

Objectives
Studying this lesson will enable students to
- use reading skills such as visualizing
- define metaphor and recognize it in two poems
- describe Naoshi Koriyama and Eve Merriam as writers
- appreciate two different approaches to reading poetry

Before Reading

Preview and Motivate
Choose from the following materials to preview the lesson and motivate your students:
____ Before Reading, *SE/ATE*, p. 505
____ Build Background, *Meeting the Standards Unit 5*, p. 72

During Reading

Teach the Selection(s)
Choose from the following resources to teach the selection(s):
____ During Reading, *SE/ATE*, pp. 506–508
____ Compare Literature: Metaphor, *Meeting the Standards Unit 5*, p. 73

Differentiate Instruction
Consider the following alternative teaching options to differentiate instruction:
____ Reading Proficiency, *ATE*, p. 507
____ Enrichment, *ATE*, p. 507
____ English Language Learning, *ATE*, p. 508
____ Lyric Poems Comparison: Poems on Poetry, *Differentiated Instruction for Advanced Students*, pp. 31–32

After Reading

Review and Extend
Use the following materials to review and extend the lesson:
____ After Reading, *SE/ATE*, pp. 507, 509
____ Compare Literature: Metaphor (continued), *Meeting the Standards Unit 5*, p. 74
____ Compare Literature: Poetic Elements, *Meeting the Standards Unit 5*, p. 75
____ Using Reading Strategies: Make Connections, *Meeting the Standards Unit 5*, p. 76
____ What Do You Think? *Meeting the Standards Unit 5*, p. 79

Assess

Administer the following assessment tool(s):

_____ Selection Quiz: Focus on "Unfolding Bud," *Meeting the Standards Unit 5*, p. 77

_____ Selection Quiz: Focus on "How to Eat a Poem," *Meeting the Standards Unit 5*, p. 78

_____ Lesson Test, *Assessment Guide*, pp. 159–160

Technology Tools

Enhance the lesson with interactive activities offered in these technology supplements:

- EMC Launchpad
- Annotated Teacher's Edition on CD
- Interactive Student Text on CD
- Exam*View*® Assessment Suite on CD
- Visual Teaching Package
- ETS Online Criterion-Based Essay Grader (Grades 9–12)
- EMC Audio Library
- EMC E-Library
- **mirrorsandwindows.com**

Name: _____ Date: _____

Haiku / *from* Lost in Translation, p. 510

Directed Reading
- **Reading Level:** Moderate
- **Difficulty Consideration:** Structure
- **Ease Factor:** Brevity and vocabulary

Pacing
- **Regular Schedule:** 1 day
- **Block Schedule:** 0.5 day

Objectives
Studying this lesson will enable students to
- use reading skills such as comparing and contrasting
- define haiku and recognize various qualities and examples of this poetic form
- describe Matsuo Bashō, Yosa Buson, and Kobayashi Issa and explain their contributions to the haiku tradition
- appreciate haiku and the intricacies of constructing it

Before Reading

Preview and Motivate
Choose from the following materials to preview the lesson and motivate your students:
_____   Before Reading, *SE/ATE*, p. 510
_____   Creative Writing: Haiku, *Meeting the Standards Unit 5*, p. 80

During Reading

Teach the Selection(s)
Choose from the following resources to teach the selection(s):
_____   During Reading, *SE/ATE*, pp. 511–512
_____   Informational Text Connection: from *Lost in Translation*, *SE/ATE*, pp. 513–514
_____   Research Skills: Find Examples, *ATE*, p. 513
_____   Analyze Literature: Form and Imagery, *Meeting the Standards Unit 5*, pp. 81–83

Differentiate Instruction
Consider the following alternative teaching options to differentiate instruction:
_____   Reading Proficiency, *ATE*, p. 512
_____   Enrichment, *ATE*, p. 512

After Reading

Review and Extend
Use the following materials to review and extend the lesson:
_____   After Reading, *SE/ATE*, pp. 512, 514
_____   Text-to-Text Connection, *Meeting the Standards Unit 5*, p. 84
_____   Art Connection: Japanese Painting, *Meeting the Standards Unit 5*, p. 85
_____   Interrupters, *Exceeding the Standards: Grammar & Style*, pp. 123–125

Assess

Administer the following assessment tool(s):

_____ Selection Quiz, *Meeting the Standards Unit 5*, p. 86

_____ Lesson Test, *Assessment Guide*, pp. 161–162

Technology Tools

Enhance the lesson with interactive activities offered in these technology supplements:

- EMC Launchpad
- Annotated Teacher's Edition on CD
- Interactive Student Text on CD
- Exam*View*® Assessment Suite on CD
- Visual Teaching Package
- ETS Online Criterion-Based Essay Grader (Grades 9–12)
- EMC Audio Library
- EMC E-Library
- **mirrorsandwindows.com**

Name: _____ Date: _____

M T W Th F

the sky was, p. 515

Directed Reading
- **Reading Level:** Moderate
- **Difficulty Consideration:** Structure and syntax
- **Ease Factor:** Intriguing shape

Pacing
- **Regular Schedule:** 1 day
- **Block Schedule:** 0.5 day

Objectives
Studying this lesson will enable students to
- use reading skills such as considering text organization
- define concrete poetry and recognize how the selection is an example of this literary technique
- infer why E. E. Cummings experimented with language
- appreciate a concrete poem expressing enjoyment

Before Reading

Preview and Motivate
Choose from the following materials to preview the lesson and motivate your students:
____ Before Reading, *SE/ATE*, p. 515
____ Vocabulary: Renaissance Man, *Meeting the Standards Unit 5*, p. 87

During Reading

Teach the Selection(s)
Choose from the following resources to teach the selection(s):
____ During Reading, *SE/ATE*, p. 516
____ Analyze Literature: Form and Meaning, *Meeting the Standards Unit 5*, p. 88

Differentiate Instruction
Consider the following alternative teaching options to differentiate instruction:
____ Reading Strategies and Skills Practice: Use Text Organization, *Differentiated Instruction for Developing Readers*, pp. 40–42

After Reading

Review and Extend
Use the following materials to review and extend the lesson:
____ After Reading, *SE/ATE*, p. 517
____ Media Literacy: Concrete Poetry, *Exceeding the Standards: Extension Activities*, p. 15

Assess
Administer the following assessment tool(s):
____ Selection Quiz, *Meeting the Standards Unit 5*, p. 89
____ Lesson Test, *Assessment Guide*, pp. 163–164

Technology Tools

Enhance the lesson with interactive activities offered in these technology supplements:

- EMC Launchpad
- Annotated Teacher's Edition on CD
- Interactive Student Text on CD
- Exam*View*® Assessment Suite on CD
- Visual Teaching Package
- ETS Online Criterion-Based Essay Grader (Grades 9–12)
- EMC Audio Library
- EMC E-Library
- **mirrorsandwindows.com**

Name: _____   Date: _____

                                                                 M   T   W   Th   F

Two People I Want to Be Like, p. 518

Independent Reading
- **Reading Level:** Moderate
- **Difficulty Consideration:** Line breaks
- **Ease Factor:** Imagery and length

Pacing
- **Regular Schedule:** 1 day
- **Block Schedule:** 0.5 day

Objectives
Studying this lesson will enable students to
- read with developing fluency
- read silently with comprehension for a sustained period of time

---

Before Reading

Preview and Motivate
Choose from the following materials to preview the lesson and motivate your students:
_____   Before Reading, *SE/ATE*, p. 518
_____   Practice Vocabulary, *Meeting the Standards Unit 5*, p. 90

During Reading

Teach the Selection(s)
Choose from the following resources to teach the selection(s):
_____   During Reading, *SE/ATE*, p. 518
_____   Answer Questions, *Meeting the Standards Unit 5*, p. 91
_____   Use Reading Strategies: Visualize, *Meeting the Standards Unit 5*, p. 92

After Reading

Review and Extend
Use the following materials to review and extend the lesson:
_____   After Reading, *SE/ATE*, p. 519
_____   Use Reading Skills: Analyze the Effects of Form on Meaning, *Meeting the Standards Unit 5*, p. 93
_____   Describe and Critique: Poetry, *Meeting the Standards Unit 5*, p. 94

Assess
Administer the following assessment tool(s):
_____   Lesson Test, *Assessment Guide*, pp. 165–166

Technology Tools

Enhance the lesson with interactive activities offered in these technology supplements:
- EMC Launchpad
- Annotated Teacher's Edition on CD
- Interactive Student Text on CD
- Exam*View*® Assessment Suite on CD
- Visual Teaching Package
- ETS Online Criterion-Based Essay Grader (Grades 9–12)
- EMC Audio Library
- EMC E-Library
- **mirrorsandwindows.com**

Name: _____ Date: _____

Miracles, p. 520

Independent Reading
- **Reading Level:** Moderate
- **Difficulty Consideration:** Line length and topic
- **Ease Factor:** Repetition

Pacing
- **Regular Schedule:** 1 day
- **Block Schedule:** 0.5 day

Objectives
Studying this lesson will enable students to
- read with developing fluency
- read silently with comprehension for a sustained period of time

---

Before Reading

Preview and Motivate
Choose from the following materials to preview the lesson and motivate your students:
_____   Before Reading, *SE/ATE*, p. 520

During Reading

Teach the Selection(s)
Choose from the following resources to teach the selection(s):
_____   During Reading, *SE/ATE*, pp. 520–521
_____   Practice Vocabulary, *Meeting the Standards Unit 5*, p. 96
_____   Analyze Literature: Imagery, *Meeting the Standards Unit 5*, p. 97

Differentiate Instruction
Consider the following alternative teaching options to differentiate instruction:
_____   Independent Reading Study: Poems by Walt Whitman, *Differentiated Instruction for Advanced Students*, p. 33

After Reading

Review and Extend
Use the following materials to review and extend the lesson:
_____   After Reading, *SE/ATE*, p. 521
_____   Analyze Literature: Imagery (continued), *Meeting the Standards Unit 5*, p. 98
_____   Using Reading Strategies: Make Connections, *Meeting the Standards Unit 5*, p. 99
_____   Describe and Critique: Poetry, *Meeting the Standards Unit 5*, pp. 100–101
_____   Prepositions and Conjunctions, *Exceeding the Standards: Grammar & Style*, pp. 113–115

Assess
Administer the following assessment tool(s):
_____   Lesson Test, *Assessment Guide*, pp. 167–168

Technology Tools

Enhance the lesson with interactive activities offered in these technology supplements:

- EMC Launchpad
- Annotated Teacher's Edition on CD
- Interactive Student Text on CD
- Exam*View*® Assessment Suite on CD
- Visual Teaching Package
- ETS Online Criterion-Based Essay Grader (Grades 9–12)
- EMC Audio Library
- EMC E-Library
- **mirrorsandwindows.com**

Name: _____ Date: _____

Early Song, p. 522

Independent Reading
- **Reading Level:** Easy
- **Difficulty Consideration:** Metaphor
- **Ease Factor:** Vocabulary

Pacing
- **Regular Schedule:** 1 day
- **Block Schedule:** 0.5 day

Objectives
Studying this lesson will enable students to
- read with developing fluency

Before Reading

Preview and Motivate
Choose from the following materials to preview the lesson and motivate your students:
_____   Before Reading, *SE/ATE*, p. 522
_____   Vocabulary of Poetry, *Meeting the Standards Unit 5*, p. 102

During Reading

Teach the Selection(s)
Choose from the following resources to teach the selection(s):
_____   During Reading, *SE/ATE*, p. 522
_____   Ask Questions, *Meeting the Standards Unit 5*, p. 103

After Reading

Review and Extend
Use the following materials to review and extend the lesson:
_____   After Reading, *SE/ATE*, p. 522
_____   Use Reading Skills: Analyze the Effects of Form on Meaning, *Meeting the Standards Unit 5*, pp. 104–105
_____   Describe and Critique: Poetry, *Meeting the Standards Unit 5*, p. 106

Assess
Administer the following assessment tool(s):
_____   Lesson Test, *Assessment Guide*, pp. 169–170

Technology Tools

Enhance the lesson with interactive activities offered in these technology supplements:
- EMC Launchpad
- Annotated Teacher's Edition on CD
- Interactive Student Text on CD
- Exam*View*® Assessment Suite on CD
- Visual Teaching Package
- ETS Online Criterion-Based Essay Grader (Grades 9–12)
- EMC Audio Library
- EMC E-Library
- **mirrorsandwindows.com**

Name: _____ Date: _____

Writing Workshop: Expository Writing—Compare-and-Contrast Essay, p. 524

Pacing
- **Regular Schedule:** 3 days
- **Block Schedule:** 1.5 days

Objectives
Participating in this lesson will help enable students to
- write an introduction that sparks the reader's interest
- write a compare-and-contrast essay that has a solid thesis statement
- write a compare-and-contrast essay that has a clear organizational pattern
- write a compare-and-contrast essay that has transitions to indicate comparisons and contrasts
- write an effective conclusion that restates the thesis

Teach the Workshop
Select from the following resources to teach the workshop:
____ Expository Writing Workshop: Compare-and-Contrast Essay, *SE/ATE*, pp. 524–529
____ Writing Skills: Using Graphic Organizers, *ATE*, p. 525
____ Speaking & Listening Skills: Monitor Comprehension While Listening, *ATE*, p. 527
____ Writing Skills: Use Management Time Lines, *ATE*, p. 529
____ Language Arts Handbook Section 4.1, The Writing Process, *SE/ATE*, pp. 888–897

Differentiate Instruction
Consider the following alternative teaching options to differentiate instruction:
____ English Language Learning and Reading Proficiency, *ATE*, p. 526
____ Reading Proficiency, *ATE*, p. 528

Review and Extend
Use the following materials to review and extend the lesson:
____ Descriptive Writing: Create an Analogy, *Exceeding the Standards: Writing*, pp. 31–38

Technology Tools
Enhance the lesson with interactive activities offered in these technology supplements:
- EMC Launchpad
- Annotated Teacher's Edition on CD
- Interactive Student Text on CD
- Exam*View*® Assessment Suite on CD
- Visual Teaching Package
- ETS Online Criterion-Based Essay Grader (Grades 9–12)
- EMC Audio Library
- EMC E-Library
- **mirrorsandwindows.com**

Name: _____ Date: _____

M   T   W   Th   F

Speaking & Listening Workshop: Giving and Actively Listening to Expository Presentations, p. 530

Pacing
- **Regular Schedule:** 2 days
- **Block Schedule:** 1 day

Objectives
Participating in this lesson will help enable students to
- plan and deliver an expository presentation that draws the listener in with an effective introduction

- plan and deliver an expository presentation that is clear, logical, and well-organized
- plan and deliver an expository presentation that has well-researched content
- plan and deliver an expository presentation that summarizes main ideas in its conclusion

Teach the Workshop
Select from the following resources to teach the workshop:
_____   Speaking & Listening Workshop: Giving and Actively Listening to Expository Presentations, *SE/ATE*, pp. 530–531
_____   Speaking & Listening Skills: Be Aware of Cultural Sensitivity, *ATE*, p. 531
_____   Language Arts Handbook Section 7.1, Verbal and Nonverbal Communication, *SE/ATE*, p. 912
_____   Language Arts Handbook Section 7.6, Public Speaking, *SE/ATE*, pp. 916–917

Review and Extend
Use the following materials to review and extend the lesson:
_____   Giving and Actively Listening to Expository Presentations, *Exceeding the Standards: Speaking & Listening*, pp. 13–16

Technology Tools
Enhance the lesson with interactive activities offered in these technology supplements:
- EMC Launchpad
- Annotated Teacher's Edition on CD
- Interactive Student Text on CD
- Exam*View*® Assessment Suite on CD
- Visual Teaching Package

- ETS Online Criterion-Based Essay Grader (Grades 9–12)
- EMC Audio Library
- EMC E-Library
- **mirrorsandwindows.com**

Program Planning Guide   © EMC Publishing, LLC

Name: _____   Date: _____

Test Practice Workshop, p. 532

Pacing • **Regular Schedule:** 1 day • **Block Schedule:** 0.5 day **Objectives** Participating in this lesson will help enable students to • write a compare-and-contrast expository essay based on a timed writing prompt	• answer standardized test questions that demonstrate revising and editing skills • answer standardized test questions that demonstrate the ability to infer from a reading

Teach the Workshop

Select from the following resources to teach the workshop:

____   Writing Skills: Expository Essay, *SE/ATE*, p. 532
____   Revising and Editing Skills, *SE/ATE*, p. 533
____   Reading Skills, *SE/ATE*, pp. 534–535
____   Test-Taking Skills: Avoid Distractors, *ATE*, p. 535
____   Language Arts Handbook Section 8.1, Preparing for Tests, *SE/ATE*, p. 921
____   Language Arts Handbook Section 8.2, Strategies for Taking Standardized Tests, *SE/ATE*, pp. 921–922
____   Language Arts Handbook Section 8.4, Answering Multiple-Choice Questions, *SE/ATE*, p. 922
____   Language Arts Handbook Section 8.8, Answering Constructed-Response Questions, *SE/ATE*, pp. 923–924
____   Language Arts Handbook Section 8.9, Answering Essay Questions, *SE/ATE*, pp. 924–925
____   Test-Taking Skills and Strategies, *Exceeding the Standards: Test Practice*, pp. 1–4

Differentiate Instruction

Consider the following alternative teaching options to differentiate instruction:

____   English Language Learning, *ATE*, p. 535

Review and Extend

Use the following materials to review and extend the lesson:

____   Poetry Study Guide: Practice Test, *Meeting the Standards Unit 5*, pp. 11–16
____   Expository Essay Practice Test: Timed Writing, *Exceeding the Standards: Test Practice*, p. 13

Technology Tools

Enhance the lesson with interactive activities offered in these technology supplements:

- ● EMC Launchpad
- ● Annotated Teacher's Edition on CD
- ● Interactive Student Text on CD
- ● Exam*View*® Assessment Suite on CD
- ● Visual Teaching Package
- ● ETS Online Criterion-Based Essay Grader (Grades 9–12)
- ∩ EMC Audio Library
- ● EMC E-Library
- ● **mirrorsandwindows.com**

LESSON PLAN

Unit 6 Poetry Opener, p. 536

Pacing
- **Regular Schedule:** 1 day
- **Block Schedule:** 0.5 day

Objectives
Studying this lesson will enable students to
- connect the theme expressed in a selection to their own lives
- question an author's use of images, symbols, and language to find meaning

---

Plan the Unit
Use the following resources to plan instruction for this unit:

_____   Unit 6 Visual Planning Guide: Unit-Based Resources, *ATE*, pp. 536A–536B

_____   Unit 6 Visual Planning Guide: Lesson-by-Lesson Resources, *ATE*, pp. 536C–536F

_____   Unit 6 Scope & Sequence Guide, *ATE*, pp. 536E–536J

_____   Unit 6 Building Vocabulary, *ATE*, pp. 536K–536L

_____   Launch the Unit, *ATE*, p. 536

Teach the Unit Opener
Choose from the following resources to teach the unit opener:

_____   Unit 6 Overview, *SE/ATE*, pp. 536–537

_____   Poetry Study Guide, *Meeting the Standards Unit 6*, pp. 1, 17

Extend the Unit
Choose from the following resources to extend the unit:

_____   For Your Reading List, *SE/ATE*, p. 593

_____   Unit 6, *Exceeding the Standards: Grammar & Style*, pp. 132–155

_____   Career Skills Development: Writing a Letter Requesting Job Information, *Exceeding the Standards: Special Topics*, pp. 24–25

_____   Unit 6, *Exceeding the Standards: Vocabulary & Spelling*, pp. 58–63

Assess
Administer the following assessment tool(s):

_____   Formative Surveys 1 and 2, *Assessment Guide*, pp. 3–20

_____   Reading Fluency Assessments, Passages 1 and 2, *Assessment Guide*, pp. 303–304

_____   Unit 6 Exam, *Assessment Guide*, pp. 273–276

Technology Tools
Enhance the lesson with interactive activities offered in these technology supplements:

- 🖉 EMC Launchpad
- 💿 Annotated Teacher's Edition on CD
- 💿 Interactive Student Text on CD
- 💿 Exam*View*® Assessment Suite on CD
- 📺 Visual Teaching Package

- 🖉 ETS Online Criterion-Based Essay Grader (Grades 9–12)
- 🎧 EMC Audio Library
- 🖉 EMC E-Library
- 🖉 **mirrorsandwindows.com**

Name: _____   Date: _____

M   T   W   Th   F

Theme in Yellow, p. 539

Grammar & Style Workshop: Simple, Compound, Complex, and Compound-Complex Sentences, p. 543

Guided Reading: Reading Model
- **Reading Level:** Moderate
- **Difficulty Consideration:** Personification
- **Ease Factor:** Vocabulary and length

Pacing
- **Regular Schedule:** 2 days
- **Block Schedule:** 1 day

Objectives
Studying this lesson will enable students to
- use reading skills such as identifying multiple levels of meaning
- analyze a poem's speaker
- describe Carl Sandburg and explain his contributions to free verse
- analyze a poem about autumn told from a surprising point of view

---

Before Reading

Preview and Motivate
Choose from the following materials to preview the lesson and motivate your students:
____   Poetry Reading Model, *SE/ATE*, p. 465
____   Before Reading, *SE/ATE*, p. 539
____   Build Vocabulary and Build Background, *Meeting the Standards Unit 6*, p. 19

During Reading

Teach the Selection(s)
Choose from the following resources to teach the selection(s):
____   During Reading, *SE/ATE*, pp. 540–541
____   Reading Skills: Identify Multiple Levels of Meaning, *ATE*, p. 541

Differentiate Instruction
Consider the following alternative teaching options to differentiate instruction:
____   Reading Strategies and Skills Practice: Visualize, *Differentiated Instruction for Developing Readers*, pp. 43–45

After Reading

Review and Extend
Use the following materials to review and extend the lesson:
____   After Reading, *SE/ATE*, p. 542
____   Creative Writing: An Autumn Memory, *Meeting the Standards Unit 6*, p. 20

Teach the Workshop(s)

Select from the following materials to teach the workshop(s):

____ Grammar & Style: Simple, Compound, Complex, and Compound-Complex Sentences, *SE/ATE*, p. 543

____ Language Arts Handbook Section 3.1, The Sentence, *SE/ATE*, pp. 852–854

____ Simple and Complete Subjects and Predicates, *Exceeding the Standards: Grammar & Style*, pp. 10–12

____ Compound Subjects, Compound Predicates, and Compound Sentences, *Exceeding the Standards: Grammar & Style*, pp. 13–15

Assess

Administer the following assessment tool(s):

____ Selection Quiz, *Meeting the Standards Unit 6*, p. 21

____ Lesson Test, *Assessment Guide*, pp. 171–172

Technology Tools

Enhance the lesson with interactive activities offered in these technology supplements:

- EMC Launchpad
- Annotated Teacher's Edition on CD
- Interactive Student Text on CD
- Exam*View*® Assessment Suite on CD
- Visual Teaching Package
- ETS Online Criterion-Based Essay Grader (Grades 9–12)
- EMC Audio Library
- EMC E-Library
- **mirrorsandwindows.com**

Name: _____   Date: _____
                                                              M   T   W   Th   F

Once by the Pacific, p. 544

Guided Reading: Reading Model
- **Reading Level:** Moderate
- **Difficulty Consideration:** Style and personification
- **Ease Factor:** Imagery and length

Pacing
- **Regular Schedule:** 1 day
- **Block Schedule:** 0.5 day

Objectives
Studying this lesson will enable students to
- use reading skills such as analyzing text organization
- explore symbolism
- discuss Robert Frost and his use of traditional poetic form
- analyze a poem about nature's fury

Before Reading

Preview and Motivate
Choose from the following materials to preview the lesson and motivate your students:
____   Poetry Reading Model, *SE/ATE*, p. 465
____   Before Reading, *SE/ATE*, p. 544
____   Build Background and Creative Writing: Mad Lib, *Meeting the Standards Unit* 6, p. 22

During Reading

Teach the Selection(s)
Choose from the following resources to teach the selection(s):
____   During Reading, *SE/ATE*, p. 545
____   Use Reading Skills: Analyze Text Organization, *Meeting the Standards Unit* 6, p. 23

After Reading

Review and Extend
Use the following materials to review and extend the lesson:
____   After Reading, *SE/ATE*, p. 546
____   Art Connection: Draw a Poem, *Meeting the Standards Unit* 6, p. 24
____   Phrases and Clauses, *Exceeding the Standards: Grammar & Style*, pp. 132–133
____   Descriptive Writing: Write a Descriptive Poem, *Exceeding the Standards: Writing*, pp. 39–46

Assess
Administer the following assessment tool(s):
____   Selection Quiz, *Meeting the Standards Unit 6*, p. 25
____   Lesson Test, *Assessment Guide*, pp. 173–174

Technology Tools

Enhance the lesson with interactive activities offered in these technology supplements:
- EMC Launchpad
- Annotated Teacher's Edition on CD
- Interactive Student Text on CD
- Exam*View*® Assessment Suite on CD
- Visual Teaching Package
- ETS Online Criterion-Based Essay Grader (Grades 9–12)
- EMC Audio Library
- EMC E-Library
- **mirrorsandwindows.com**

LESSON PLAN

Name: _____   Date: _____

Annabel Lee / The Highwayman, p. 547

Directed Reading
"Annabel Lee"
- **Reading Level:** Moderate
- **Difficulty Consideration:** Older English and vocabulary
- **Ease Factor:** Compelling story, fairy tale style

"The Highwayman"
- **Reading Level:** Challenging
- **Difficulty Consideration:** Many footnotes, adult concepts
- **Ease Factor:** Rhymes, suspenseful

Pacing
- **Regular Schedule:** 1 day
- **Block Schedule:** 0.5 day

Objectives
Studying this lesson will enable students to
- analyze narrative poetry and compare two examples
- describe the literary accomplishments of Edgar Allan Poe and Alfred Noyes
- appreciate two poems about love that transcends death

Before Reading

Preview and Motivate
Choose from the following materials to preview the lesson and motivate your students:
____   Before Reading, *SE/ATE*, p. 547
____   Build Background, Set Purpose, Practice Vocabulary, *Meeting the Standards Unit 6*, p. 26

During Reading

Teach the Selection(s)
Choose from the following resources to teach the selection(s):
____   During Reading, *SE/ATE*, pp. 548–555
____   Cultural Connection: Gothic Literature, *SE/ATE*, p. 550
____   Reading Skills: Identify Sequence of Events, *ATE*, p. 549
____   Speaking & Listening Skills: Choral Reading, *ATE*, p. 553
____   Reading Skills: Compare and Contrast, *ATE*, p. 555
____   Compare Literature: Narrative Poetry, *Meeting the Standards Unit 6*, p. 27

Differentiate Instruction
Consider the following alternative teaching options to differentiate instruction:
____   English Language Learning, *ATE*, pp. 550, 552
____   Reading Proficiency, *ATE*, p. 552
____   Auditory Learning, *ATE*, p. 552
____   Enrichment, *ATE*, p. 554
____   Understand Literary Elements: Mood, *Differentiated Instruction for English Language Learners,* pp. 139–145

After Reading

Review and Extend

Use the following materials to review and extend the lesson:

_____   After Reading, *SE/ATE*, pp. 550, 556

_____   Compare Literature: Narrative Poetry (continued), *Meeting the Standards Unit 6*, p. 28

_____   Compare Literature: Word Choice, *Meeting the Standards Unit 6*, p. 29

_____   Use Reading Strategies: Make Connections, *Meeting the Standards Unit 6*, p. 30

_____   What Do You Think? *Meeting the Standards Unit 6*, p. 34

_____   Lifelong Learning: Write a Literary Critique, *Exceeding the Standards: Extension Activities*, pp. 16–17

_____   Prepositional Phrases, *Exceeding the Standards: Grammar & Style*, pp. 134–136

_____   Types of Clauses within a Sentence, *Exceeding the Standards: Grammar & Style*, pp. 144–150

Assess

Administer the following assessment tool(s):

_____   Selection Quiz: Focus on "Annabel Lee," *Meeting the Standards Unit 6*, pp. 31–32

_____   Selection Quiz: Focus on "The Highwayman," *Meeting the Standards Unit 6*, p. 33

_____   Lesson Test, *Assessment Guide*, pp. 175–176

Technology Tools

Enhance the lesson with interactive activities offered in these technology supplements:

- EMC Launchpad
- Annotated Teacher's Edition on CD
- Interactive Student Text on CD
- Exam*View*® Assessment Suite on CD
- Visual Teaching Package
- ETS Online Criterion-Based Essay Grader (Grades 9–12)
- EMC Audio Library
- EMC E-Library
- **mirrorsandwindows.com**

Name: _____ Date: _____

The Filling Station, p. 557

Vocabulary & Spelling Workshop: Figurative Language, p. 561

Directed Reading
- **Reading Level:** Moderate
- **Difficulty Consideration:** Vocabulary
- **Ease Factor:** Sensory details

Pacing
- **Regular Schedule:** 1 day
- **Block Schedule:** 0.5 day

Objectives
Studying this lesson will enable students to
- use reading skills such as identifying the main idea
- explore tone
- describe Elizabeth Bishop and appreciate the vivid images she creates
- analyze a poem to find meaning below the surface of an ordinary place

---

Before Reading

Preview and Motivate
Choose from the following materials to preview the lesson and motivate your students:
____   Before Reading, *SE/ATE*, p. 557
____   Creative Writing: Memory Poem, *Meeting the Standards Unit 6*, p. 35

During Reading

Teach the Selection(s)
Choose from the following resources to teach the selection(s):
____   During Reading, *SE/ATE*, p. 559
____   Analyze Literature: Figurative Language and Irony, *Meeting the Standards Unit 6*, p. 36

Differentiate Instruction
Consider the following alternative teaching options to differentiate instruction:
____   English Language Learning, *ATE*, p. 559
____   Reading Proficiency, *ATE*, p. 559

After Reading

Review and Extend
Use the following materials to review and extend the lesson:
____   After Reading, *SE/ATE*, p. 560
____   Math Connection, *Meeting the Standards Unit 6*, p. 37
____   Media Literacy: Draw the Images, *Exceeding the Standards: Extension Activities*, p. 18

Teach the Workshop(s)
Select from the following materials to teach the workshop(s):
____   Vocabulary & Spelling: Figurative Language, *SE/ATE*, p. 561
____   Figurative Language, *Exceeding the Standards: Vocabulary & Spelling*, pp. 71–73

Assess

Administer the following assessment tool(s):

_____ Selection Quiz, *Meeting the Standards Unit 6*, pp. 38–39

_____ Lesson Test, *Assessment Guide*, pp. 177–178

Technology Tools

Enhance the lesson with interactive activities offered in these technology supplements:

- EMC Launchpad
- Annotated Teacher's Edition on CD
- Interactive Student Text on CD
- Exam*View*® Assessment Suite on CD
- Visual Teaching Package
- ETS Online Criterion-Based Essay Grader (Grades 9–12)
- EMC Audio Library
- EMC E-Library
- **mirrorsandwindows.com**

Name Giveaway / *from* An Indian Boy's Story, p. 562

Vocabulary & Spelling Workshop: Spelling by Syllables, p. 567

Directed Reading
- **Reading Level:** Easy
- **Difficulty Consideration:** Topic
- **Ease Factor:** Vocabulary

Pacing
- **Regular Schedule:** 2 days
- **Block Schedule:** 1 day

Objectives

Studying this lesson will enable students to
- use reading skills to analyze and understand text organization
- identify elements of a lyric poem
- connect literature to social studies
- synthesize content from different texts

Before Reading

Preview and Motivate

Choose from the following materials to preview the lesson and motivate your students:

____ Before Reading, *SE/ATE*, p. 562

____ Build Background, *Meeting the Standards Unit 6*, pp. 40–41

During Reading

Teach the Selection(s)

Choose from the following resources to teach the selection(s):

____ During Reading, *SE/ATE*, p. 563

____ Primary Source Connection: from *An Indian Boy's Story*, *SE/ATE*, pp. 564–565

____ Vocabulary Skills: Word Meanings, *SE/ATE*, p. 565

____ Analyze Literature: Lyric Poetry, *Meeting the Standards Unit 6*, p. 42

Differentiate Instruction

Consider the following alternative teaching options to differentiate instruction:

____ Enrichment, *ATE*, p. 564

____ Historical Context Project: Native American Culture versus Assimilation, *Differentiated Instruction for Advanced Students*, pp. 34–35

After Reading

Review and Extend

Use the following materials to review and extend the lesson:

____ After Reading, *SE/ATE*, pp. 563, 566

____ Make Connections, *Meeting the Standards Unit 6*, p. 43

____ Lifelong Learning: Making Good Choices: Part 2, *Exceeding the Standards: Special Topics*, pp. 22–23

Teach the Workshop(s)

Select from the following materials to teach the workshop(s):

____ Vocabulary & Spelling: Spelling by Syllables, *SE/ATE*, p. 567
____ Language Arts Handbook Section 2.7, *SE/ATE*, pp. 843–851
____ Syllabication, *Exceeding the Standards: Vocabulary & Spelling*, pp. 13–14
____ Spelling by Syllables, *Exceeding the Standards: Vocabulary & Spelling*, pp. 15–16
____ Syllables Review, *Exceeding the Standards: Vocabulary & Spelling*, p. 20

Assess

Administer the following assessment tool(s):

____ Selection Quiz, *Meeting the Standards Unit 6*, p. 44
____ Lesson Test, *Assessment Guide*, pp. 179–180

Technology Tools

Enhance the lesson with interactive activities offered in these technology supplements:

- EMC Launchpad
- Annotated Teacher's Edition on CD
- Interactive Student Text on CD
- Exam*View*® Assessment Suite on CD
- Visual Teaching Package
- ETS Online Criterion-Based Essay Grader (Grades 9–12)
- EMC Audio Library
- EMC E-Library
- **mirrorsandwindows.com**

Name: _____ Date: _____
                                                                 M   T   W   Th   F

Ancestors, p. 568

Grammar & Style Workshop: Simple, Complete, and Compound Predicates, p. 571

Directed Reading
- **Reading Level:** Easy
- **Difficulty Consideration:** None
- **Ease Factor:** Vocabulary and topic

Pacing
- **Regular Schedule:** 1 day
- **Block Schedule:** 0.5 day

Objectives
Studying this lesson will enable students to
- use reading skills such as analyzing main idea and supporting details
- explore author's purpose
- describe Dudley Randall and analyze his use of free verse
- analyze a poem about ancestry

Before Reading

Preview and Motivate
Choose from the following materials to preview the lesson and motivate your students:
_____ Before Reading, *SE/ATE*, p. 568
_____ Career Connection, *Meeting the Standards Unit 6*, p. 45
_____ Cultural Connection: Genealogy, *Meeting the Standards Unit 6*, p. 46

During Reading

Teach the Selection(s)
Choose from the following resources to teach the selection(s):
_____ During Reading, *SE/ATE*, p. 569
_____ Use Reading Skills: Drawing Conclusions, *Meeting the Standards Unit 6*, p. 47

Differentiate Instruction
Consider the following alternative teaching options to differentiate instruction:
_____ Cultural Connection Activity: From African to African American, *Differentiated Instruction for Advanced Students*, pp. 36–37

After Reading

Review and Extend
Use the following materials to review and extend the lesson:
_____ After Reading, *SE/ATE*, p. 570
_____ Extend Understanding: Creative Writing, *Meeting the Standards Unit 6*, p. 48

Teach the Workshop(s)
Select from the following materials to teach the workshop(s):
_____ Grammar & Style: Simple, Complete, and Compound Predicates, *SE/ATE*, p. 571
_____ Language Arts Handbook Section 3.1, The Sentence, *SE/ATE*, pp. 852–854
_____ Simple and Complete Subjects and Predicates, *Exceeding the Standards: Grammar & Style*, pp. 10–12
_____ Compound Subjects, Compound Predicates, and Compound Sentences, *Exceeding the Standards: Grammar & Style*, pp. 13–15

Assess

Administer the following assessment tool(s):

_____ Selection Quiz, *Meeting the Standards Unit 6*, p. 49

_____ Lesson Test, *Assessment Guide*, pp. 181–182

Technology Tools

Enhance the lesson with interactive activities offered in these technology supplements:

- EMC Launchpad
- Annotated Teacher's Edition on CD
- Interactive Student Text on CD
- Exam*View*® Assessment Suite on CD
- Visual Teaching Package
- ETS Online Criterion-Based Essay Grader (Grades 9–12)
- EMC Audio Library
- EMC E-Library
- **mirrorsandwindows.com**

Name: _____ Date: _____

M   T   W   Th   F

The Lost Parrot, p. 572

Directed Reading
- **Reading Level:** Easy
- **Difficulty Consideration:** None
- **Ease Factor:** Vocabulary

Pacing
- **Regular Schedule:** 1 day
- **Block Schedule:** 0.5 day

Objectives
Studying this lesson will enable students to
- use reading skills such as compare and contrast
- analyze symbols
- describe Naomi Shihab Nye and discuss how she expresses her observations
- appreciate a poem about loss and hope

Before Reading

Preview and Motivate
Choose from the following materials to preview the lesson and motivate your students:
_____   Before Reading, *SE/ATE*, p. 572
_____   Science Connection, *Meeting the Standards Unit 6*, p. 50
_____   Creative Writing: Diamante, *Meeting the Standards Unit 6*, p. 51

During Reading

Teach the Selection(s)
Choose from the following resources to teach the selection(s):
_____   During Reading, *SE/ATE*, pp. 573–574
_____   Analyze Literature: Characterization, *Meeting the Standards Unit 6*, p. 52
_____   Use Reading Strategies: Ask Questions, *Meeting the Standards Unit 6*, p. 53

Differentiate Instruction
Consider the following alternative teaching options to differentiate instruction:
_____   Reading Proficiency, *ATE*, p. 574
_____   Reading Strategies and Skills Practice: Take Notes, *Differentiated Instruction for Developing Readers*, pp. 46–48

After Reading

Review and Extend
Use the following materials to review and extend the lesson:
_____   After Reading, *SE/ATE*, p. 575
_____   Creative Writing: "Lost Pet" Poster, *Meeting the Standards Unit 6*, p. 54

Assess
Administer the following assessment tool(s):
_____   Selection Quiz, *Meeting the Standards Unit 6*, p. 55
_____   Lesson Test, *Assessment Guide*, pp. 183–184

Technology Tools

Enhance the lesson with interactive activities offered in these technology supplements:

- EMC Launchpad
- Annotated Teacher's Edition on CD
- Interactive Student Text on CD
- Exam*View*® Assessment Suite on CD
- Visual Teaching Package
- ETS Online Criterion-Based Essay Grader (Grades 9–12)
- EMC Audio Library
- EMC E-Library
- **mirrorsandwindows.com**

Name: _____ Date: _____

M   T   W   Th   F

For My Father, p. 576

Directed Reading
- **Reading Level:** Moderate
- **Difficulty Consideration:** Figurative language and background
- **Ease Factor:** Vocabulary

Pacing
- **Regular Schedule:** 1 day
- **Block Schedule:** 0.5 day

Objectives
Studying this lesson will enable students to
- use reading skills such as analyzing text structure
- identify hyperbole
- describe Janice Mirikitani and discuss her use of strong emotions in her work
- appreciate a poem about harsh realities

Before Reading

Preview and Motivate
Choose from the following materials to preview the lesson and motivate your students:
_____   Before Reading, *SE/ATE*, p. 576
_____   Build Background, *Meeting the Standards Unit 6*, p. 56

During Reading

Teach the Selection(s)
Choose from the following resources to teach the selection(s):
_____   During Reading, *SE/ATE*, pp. 577–578
_____   History Connection: Japanese Internment, *SE/ATE*, p. 578
_____   Make Judgments, *Meeting the Standards Unit 6*, p. 57

Differentiate Instruction
Consider the following alternative teaching options to differentiate instruction:
_____   Reading Proficiency, *ATE*, p. 578
_____   Character Analysis Study: Two Faces of Immigrants, *Differentiated Instruction for Advanced Students*, pp. 38–39

After Reading

Review and Extend
Use the following materials to review and extend the lesson:
_____   After Reading, *SE/ATE*, p. 579
_____   Describe and Critique, *Meeting the Standards Unit 6*, pp. 58–59

Assess
Administer the following assessment tool(s):
_____   Selection Quiz, *Meeting the Standards Unit 6*, p. 60
_____   Lesson Test, *Assessment Guide*, pp. 185–186

Technology Tools

Enhance the lesson with interactive activities offered in these technology supplements:

- EMC Launchpad
- Annotated Teacher's Edition on CD
- Interactive Student Text on CD
- Exam*View*® Assessment Suite on CD
- Visual Teaching Package
- ETS Online Criterion-Based Essay Grader (Grades 9–12)
- EMC Audio Library
- EMC E-Library
- **mirrorsandwindows.com**

Name: _____ Date: _____

Money Order / Sisters, p. 580

Directed Reading
- **Reading Level:** Easy
- **Difficulty Consideration:** Irony and metaphor
- **Ease Factor:** Length and vocabulary

Pacing
- **Regular Schedule:** 2 days
- **Block Schedule:** 1 day

Objectives
Studying this lesson will enable students to
- use reading skills such as evaluating cause and effect
- analyze irony
- describe the literary accomplishments of Janet Wong and discuss her use of imagery
- appreciate two poems about family relationships

Before Reading

Preview and Motivate
Choose from the following materials to preview the lesson and motivate your students:
_____   Before Reading, *SE/ATE*, p. 580
_____   Cultural Connections: Foods of the World, *Meeting the Standards Unit 6*, pp. 61–62

During Reading

Teach the Selection(s)
Choose from the following resources to teach the selection(s):
_____   During Reading, *SE/ATE*, pp. 581–582
_____   Grammar Skills, *ATE*, p. 581
_____   Analyze Literature: Symbolism and Irony, *Meeting the Standards Unit 6*, pp. 63–65

Differentiate Instruction
Consider the following alternative teaching options to differentiate instruction:
_____   Reading Proficiency, *ATE*, p. 582

After Reading

Review and Extend
Use the following materials to review and extend the lesson:
_____   After Reading, *SE/ATE*, p. 583

Assess
Administer the following assessment tool(s):
_____   Selection Quiz, *Meeting the Standards Unit 6*, p. 66
_____   Lesson Test, *Assessment Guide*, pp. 187–188

Technology Tools

Enhance the lesson with interactive activities offered in these technology supplements:

- EMC Launchpad
- Annotated Teacher's Edition on CD
- Interactive Student Text on CD
- Exam*View*® Assessment Suite on CD
- Visual Teaching Package
- ETS Online Criterion-Based Essay Grader (Grades 9–12)
- EMC Audio Library
- EMC E-Library
- **mirrorsandwindows.com**

Name: _____   Date: _____
M   T   W   Th   F

I'm Nobody, p. 584

Independent Reading
- **Reading Level:** Easy
- **Difficulty Consideration:** Metaphor
- **Ease Factor:** Length

Pacing
- **Regular Schedule:** 1 day
- **Block Schedule:** 0.5 day

Objectives
Studying this lesson will enable students to
- read with developing fluency
- read silently with comprehension

Before Reading

Preview and Motivate
Choose from the following materials to preview the lesson and motivate your students:
_____ Before Reading, *SE/ATE*, p. 584
_____ Vocabulary: Multiple Meaning Words, *Meeting the Standards Unit 6*, pp. 67–68

During Reading

Teach the Selection(s)
Choose from the following resources to teach the selection(s):
_____ During Reading, *SE/ATE*, p. 584
_____ Analyze Literature: Simile and Metaphor, *Meeting the Standards Unit 6*, p. 69

Differentiate Instruction
Consider the following alternative teaching options to differentiate instruction:
_____ Compare and Contrast, *Differentiated Instruction for English Language Learners*, pp. 146–151

After Reading

Review and Extend
Use the following materials to review and extend the lesson:
_____ After Reading, *SE/ATE*, p. 585
_____ Analyze Literature: Tone, *Meeting the Standards Unit 6*, p. 70
_____ Analyze Literature: Speaker, *Meeting the Standards Unit 6*, p. 71
_____ Describe and Critique: Poetry, *Meeting the Standards Unit 6*, pp. 72–73

Assess
Administer the following assessment tool(s):
_____ Lesson Test, *Assessment Guide*, pp. 189–190

Technology Tools

Enhance the lesson with interactive activities offered in these technology supplements:

- EMC Launchpad
- Annotated Teacher's Edition on CD
- Interactive Student Text on CD
- Exam*View*® Assessment Suite on CD
- Visual Teaching Package
- ETS Online Criterion-Based Essay Grader (Grades 9–12)
- EMC Audio Library
- EMC E-Library
- **mirrorsandwindows.com**

Name: _____ Date: _____
M   T   W   Th   F

Refugee Ship, p. 586

Independent Reading
- **Reading Level:** Easy
- **Difficulty Consideration:** Topic
- **Ease Factor:** Vocabulary

Pacing
- **Regular Schedule:** 1 day
- **Block Schedule:** 0.5 day

Objectives
Studying this lesson will enable students to
- read with developing fluency
- read silently with comprehension

Before Reading

Preview and Motivate
Choose from the following materials to preview the lesson and motivate your students:
____   Before Reading, *SE/ATE*, p. 586
____   Vocabulary: Multiple Meaning Words, *Meeting the Standards Unit 6*, pp. 67–68

During Reading

Teach the Selection(s)
Choose from the following resources to teach the selection(s):
____   During Reading, *SE/ATE*, p. 586
____   Analyze Literature: Simile and Metaphor, *Meeting the Standards Unit 6*, p. 69

After Reading

Review and Extend
Use the following materials to review and extend the lesson:
____   After Reading, *SE/ATE*, p. 587
____   Analyze Literature: Tone, *Meeting the Standards Unit 6*, p. 70
____   Analyze Literature: Speaker, *Meeting the Standards Unit 6*, p. 71
____   Describe and Critique: Poetry, *Meeting the Standards Unit 6*, pp. 72–73
____   Verbal Phrases, *Exceeding the Standards: Grammar & Style*, pp. 137–139

Assess
Administer the following assessment tool(s):
____   Lesson Test, *Assessment Guide*, pp. 191–192

Technology Tools

Enhance the lesson with interactive activities offered in these technology supplements:
- EMC Launchpad
- Annotated Teacher's Edition on CD
- Interactive Student Text on CD
- Exam*View*® Assessment Suite on CD
- Visual Teaching Package
- ETS Online Criterion-Based Essay Grader (Grades 9–12)
- EMC Audio Library
- EMC E-Library
- **mirrorsandwindows.com**

Name: _____ Date: _____

Literary Element: Understanding Meaning in Poetry, p. 538

Loo Wit, p. 588

Independent Reading
- **Reading Level:** Moderate
- **Difficulty Consideration:** Topic and imagery
- **Ease Factor:** Vocabulary

Pacing
- **Regular Schedule:** 1 day
- **Block Schedule:** 0.5 day

Objectives
Studying this lesson will enable students to
- read with developing fluency
- read silently with comprehension

Before Reading

Teach the Feature(s)
Select from the following resources to teach the feature(s):
____   Literary Element: Understanding Meaning in Poetry, *SE/ATE*, p. 538
____   Understanding and Applying Meaning in Poetry to the Selections, *Meeting the Standards Unit 6*, pp. 2–4
____   Analyze Poetry, *Exceeding the Standards: Literature & Reading*, pp. 14–16

Preview and Motivate
Choose from the following materials to preview the lesson and motivate your students:
____   Before Reading, *SE/ATE*, p. 588
____   Practice Vocabulary, *Meeting the Standards Unit 6*, p. 74

During Reading

Teach the Selection(s)
Choose from the following resources to teach the selection(s):
____   During Reading, *SE/ATE*, pp. 588–589
____   Science Connection: Mount Saint Helens, *SE/ATE*, p. 590
____   Analyze Poetry: Sequence and Figurative Language, *Meeting the Standards Unit 6*, p. 75

Differentiate Instruction
Consider the following alternative teaching options to differentiate instruction:
____   Enrichment, *ATE*, p. 590
____   Independent Reading Project: Natural Catastrophes That Changed the World, *Differentiated Instruction for Advanced Students*, p. 40

After Reading

Review and Extend

Use the following materials to review and extend the lesson:

_____ After Reading, *SE/ATE*, p. 590

_____ Analyze Poetry: Compare and Contrast, *Meeting the Standards Unit 6*, p. 76

_____ Enrichment: Dialogue Between Speakers, *Meeting the Standards Unit 6*, pp. 77–78

_____ Describe and Critique: Poetry, *Meeting the Standards Unit 6*, pp. 79–80

Assess

Administer the following assessment tool(s):

_____ Lesson Test, *Assessment Guide*, pp. 193–194

Technology Tools

Enhance the lesson with interactive activities offered in these technology supplements:

- EMC Launchpad
- Annotated Teacher's Edition on CD
- Interactive Student Text on CD
- Exam*View*® Assessment Suite on CD
- Visual Teaching Package
- ETS Online Criterion-Based Essay Grader (Grades 9–12)
- EMC Audio Library
- EMC E-Library
- **mirrorsandwindows.com**

Name: _____ Date: _____

The Pasture, p. 591

Independent Reading
- **Reading Level:** Easy
- **Difficulty Consideration:** Topic
- **Ease Factor:** Vocabulary and length

Objectives
Studying this lesson will enable students to
- read with developing fluency
- read silently with comprehension

Pacing
- **Regular Schedule:** 1 day
- **Block Schedule:** 0.5 day

Before Reading

Preview and Motivate
Choose from the following materials to preview the lesson and motivate your students:
____   Before Reading, *SE/ATE*, p. 591
____   Practice Vocabulary, *Meeting the Standards Unit 6*, p. 74

During Reading

Teach the Selection(s)
Choose from the following resources to teach the selection(s):
____   During Reading, *SE/ATE*, p. 591
____   Analyze Poetry: Sequence and Figurative Language, *Meeting the Standards Unit 6*, p. 75

After Reading

Review and Extend
Use the following materials to review and extend the lesson:
____   After Reading, *SE/ATE*, p. 592
____   Analyze Poetry: Compare and Contrast, *Meeting the Standards Unit 6*, p. 76
____   Enrichment: Dialogue Between Speakers, *Meeting the Standards Unit 6*, pp. 77–78
____   Describe and Critique: Poetry, *Meeting the Standards Unit 6*, pp. 79–80
____   Types of Clauses within a Sentence, *Exceeding the Standards: Grammar & Style*, pp. 144–150

Assess
Administer the following assessment tool(s):
____   Lesson Test, *Assessment Guide*, pp. 195–196

Technology Tools

Enhance the lesson with interactive activities offered in these technology supplements:

- EMC Launchpad
- Annotated Teacher's Edition on CD
- Interactive Student Text on CD
- Exam*View*® Assessment Suite on CD
- Visual Teaching Package

- ETS Online Criterion-Based Essay Grader (Grades 9–12)
- EMC Audio Library
- EMC E-Library
- **mirrorsandwindows.com**

Name: _____ Date: _____

M   T   W   Th   F

Writing Workshop: Narrative Writing—Personal Narrative, p. 594

Pacing
- **Regular Schedule:** 3 days
- **Block Schedule:** 1.5 days

Objectives
Participating in this lesson will help enable students to
- write a personal narrative that grabs the reader's attention
- write a personal narrative that is organized by sequence of events
- write a personal narrative that includes descriptive detail as well as personal thoughts and feeling
- write a personal narrative that makes an event's significance clear in a compelling conclusion

Teach the Workshop
Select from the following resources to teach the workshop:
_____   Writing Workshop: Narrative Writing—Personal Narrative, *SE/ATE*, pp. 594–599
_____   Reading Skills: Identify Author's Approach, *ATE*, p. 595
_____   Speaking and Listening Skills: Retell and Summarize Points, *ATE*, p. 597
_____   Writing Skills: Refer to Prewriting Plan, *ATE*, p. 599
_____   Language Arts Handbook Section 4.1, The Writing Process, *SE/ATE*, pp. 888–897
_____   Language Arts Handbook Section 4.2, Modes and Purposes of Writing, *SE/ATE*, p. 887

Differentiate Instruction
Consider the following alternative teaching options to differentiate instruction:
_____   Reading Proficiency, *ATE*, p. 596
_____   English Language Learning, *ATE*, p. 598
_____   Enrichment, *ATE*, p. 598

Review and Extend
Use the following materials to review and extend the lesson:
_____   Descriptive Writing: Write a Descriptive Poem, *Exceeding the Standards: Writing*, pp. 39–46

Technology Tools
Enhance the lesson with interactive activities offered in these technology supplements:
- EMC Launchpad
- Annotated Teacher's Edition on CD
- Interactive Student Text on CD
- Exam*View*® Assessment Suite on CD
- Visual Teaching Package
- ETS Online Criterion-Based Essay Grader (Grades 9–12)
- EMC Audio Library
- EMC E-Library
- **mirrorsandwindows.com**

Name: _____   Date: _____

Speaking & Listening Workshop: Giving and Actively Listening to Narrative Presentations, p. 600

Pacing
- **Regular Schedule:** 2 days
- **Block Schedule:** 1 day

Objectives
Participating in this lesson will help enable students to
- deliver narrative presentations that use chronological order
- deliver narrative presentations that include characters, setting, and action

- deliver narrative presentations that convey ideas through description
- deliver narrative presentations that use the voice to portray feelings
- deliver narrative presentations that are loud and clear
- deliver narrative presentations that employ effective nonverbal cues

Teach the Workshop
Select from the following resources to teach the workshop:

_____   Speaking & Listening Workshop: Giving and Actively Listening to Narrative Presentations, *SE/ATE*, pp. 600–601

_____   Writing Skills: Effective Transitions, *ATE*, p. 601

_____   Language Arts Handbook Section 7.1, Verbal and Nonverbal Communication, *SE/ATE*, p. 912

_____   Language Arts Handbook Section 7.2, Listening Skills, *SE/ATE*, pp. 913–914

_____   Language Arts Handbook Section 7.6, Public Speaking, *SE/ATE*, pp. 916–917

_____   Language Arts Handbook Section 7.8, Telling a Story, *SE/ATE*, pp. 918–919

Differentiate Instruction
Consider the following alternative teaching options to differentiate instruction:

_____   English Language Learning, *ATE*, p. 600

Review and Extend
Use the following materials to review and extend the lesson:

_____   Giving and Actively Listening to Narrative Presentations, *Exceeding the Standards: Speaking & Listening*, pp. 17–18

Technology Tools
Enhance the lesson with interactive activities offered in these technology supplements:

- EMC Launchpad
- Annotated Teacher's Edition on CD
- Interactive Student Text on CD
- Exam*View*® Assessment Suite on CD
- Visual Teaching Package

- ETS Online Criterion-Based Essay Grader (Grades 9–12)
- EMC Audio Library
- EMC E-Library
- **mirrorsandwindows.com**

Name: _____ Date: _____

Test Practice Workshop, p. 602

Pacing
- **Regular Schedule:** 1 day
- **Block Schedule:** 0.5 day

Objectives
Participating in this lesson will help enable students to
- write a personal essay based on a timed writing prompt

- answer standardized test questions that demonstrate revising and editing skills
- answer standardized test questions that demonstrate the ability to infer from a reading

Teach the Workshop
Select from the following resources to teach the workshop:
_____ Writing Skills: Personal Essay, *SE/ATE*, p. 602
_____ Revising and Editing Skills, *SE/ATE*, p. 603
_____ Reading Skills, *SE/ATE*, pp. 604–605
_____ Test-Taking Skills: Eliminate Incorrect Responses, *ATE*, p. 605
_____ Language Arts Handbook Section 8.1, Preparing for Tests, *SE/ATE*, p. 921
_____ Language Arts Handbook Section 8.2, Strategies for Taking Standardized Tests, *SE/ATE*, pp. 921–922
_____ Language Arts Handbook Section 8.4, Answering Multiple-Choice Questions, *SE/ATE*, p. 922
_____ Language Arts Handbook Section 8.5, Answering Reading Comprehension Questions, *SE/ATE*, p. 923
_____ Language Arts Handbook Section 8.9, Answering Essay Questions, *SE/ATE*, pp. 924–925
_____ Test-Taking Skills and Strategies, *Exceeding the Standards: Test Practice*, pp. 1–4

Differentiate Instruction
Consider the following alternative teaching options to differentiate instruction:
_____ English Language Learning, *ATE*, p. 604

Review and Extend
Use the following materials to review and extend the lesson:
_____ Practice Test, *Meeting the Standards Unit 6*, pp. 11–16
_____ Personal Essay Practice Test: Revising and Editing, *Exceeding the Standards: Writing*, pp. 14–15

Technology Tools
Enhance the lesson with interactive activities offered in these technology supplements:
- EMC Launchpad
- Annotated Teacher's Edition on CD
- Interactive Student Text on CD
- Exam*View*® Assessment Suite on CD
- Visual Teaching Package
- ETS Online Criterion-Based Essay Grader (Grades 9–12)
- EMC Audio Library
- EMC E-Library
- **mirrorsandwindows.com**

Name: _____ Date: _____

Unit 7 Drama Opener, p. 606

Pacing
- **Regular Schedule:** 1 day
- **Block Schedule:** 0.5 day

Objectives
Studying this lesson will enable students to
- connect the theme expressed in a selection to their own lives
- identify common forms of drama
- understand different elements of drama

Plan the Unit

Use the following resources to plan instruction for this unit:

_____ Unit 7 Visual Planning Guide: Unit-Based Resources, *ATE*, pp. 606A–606B

_____ Unit 7 Visual Planning Guide: Lesson-by-Lesson Resources, *ATE*, pp. 606C–606D

_____ Unit 7 Scope & Sequence Guide, *ATE*, pp. 606E–606H

_____ Unit 7 Building Vocabulary, *ATE*, pp. 606I–606J

_____ Launch the Unit, *ATE*, p. 606

Teach the Unit Opener

Choose from the following resources to teach the unit opener:

_____ Unit 7 Overview, *SE/ATE*, pp. 606–607

_____ Introduction to Drama, *SE/ATE*, pp. 608–609

_____ Drama Study Guide: Introduction, *Meeting the Standards Unit 7*, p. 1

_____ Drama Study Guide: Introduction to Drama and Applying Drama to the Selections, *Meeting the Standards Unit 7*, pp. 2–10

_____ Drama Study Guide: Master Vocabulary List, *Meeting the Standards Unit 7*, p. 17

Differentiate Instruction

Consider the following alternative teaching options to differentiate instruction:

_____ English Language Learning, *ATE*, p. 609

Extend the Unit

Choose from the following resources to extend the unit:

_____ For Your Reading List, *SE/ATE*, p. 709

_____ Unit 7, *Exceeding the Standards: Grammar & Style*, pp. 156–185

_____ Dramatize an Original Script, *Exceeding the Standards: Literature & Reading*, pp. 17–20

_____ Lifelong Learning: Setting Goals: Part 1, *Exceeding the Standards: Special Topics*, pp. 26–27

_____ Career Skills Development: Writing an Ad for Bestworkerqualities.com, *Exceeding the Standards: Special Topics*, pp. 28–30

_____ Unit 7, *Exceeding the Standards: Vocabulary & Spelling*, pp. 64–70

Assess

Administer the following assessment tool(s):

_____ Formative Surveys 1 and 2, *Assessment Guide*, pp. 3–20

_____ Reading Fluency Assessments, Passages 1 and 2, *Assessment Guide*, pp. 305–306

_____ Unit 7 Exam, *Assessment Guide*, pp. 277–280

Technology Tools

Enhance the lesson with interactive activities offered in these technology supplements:

- EMC Launchpad
- Annotated Teacher's Edition on CD
- Interactive Student Text on CD
- Exam*View*® Assessment Suite on CD
- Visual Teaching Package
- ETS Online Criterion-Based Essay Grader (Grades 9–12)
- EMC Audio Library
- EMC E-Library
- **mirrorsandwindows.com**

Name: _____ Date: _____

                                                       M   T   W   Th   F

A Defenseless Creature, p. 611

Guided Reading: Reading Model
- **Reading Level:** Moderate
- **Difficulty Consideration:** Vocabulary and characterizations
- **Ease Factor:** Humor

Pacing
- **Regular Schedule:** 3 days
- **Block Schedule:** 1.5 days

Objectives
Studying this lesson will enable students to
- use reading skills such as identifying cause and effect
- define drama and recognize elements of drama in the selection
- describe some of Neil Simon's literary accomplishments
- appreciate a humorous play based on a short story by Anton Chekhov

Before Reading

Preview and Motivate
Choose from the following materials to preview the lesson and motivate your students:
____ Drama Reading Model, *SE/ATE*, p. 610
____ Before Reading, *SE/ATE*, p. 611
____ How to Read Drama, *Meeting the Standards Unit 7*, pp. 19–20
____ Build Background: A Role-Play, *Meeting the Standards Unit 7*, p. 21
____ Vocabulary: Word Families, *Meeting the Standards Unit 7*, pp. 22–23

During Reading

Teach the Selection(s)
Choose from the following resources to teach the selection(s):
____ During Reading, *SE/ATE*, pp. 612–620
____ Writing Skills: Summarize, *ATE*, p. 615
____ Grammar Skills: Adverb Phrases, *ATE*, p. 617
____ Reading Skills: Identify Author's Perspective, *ATE*, p. 619
____ Analyze Literature: Farce, *Meeting the Standards Unit 7*, p. 24
____ Analyze Literature: Dramatic Irony, *Meeting the Standards Unit 7*, p. 25

Differentiate Instruction
Consider the following alternative teaching options to differentiate instruction:
____ English Language Learning, *ATE*, pp. 613, 614
____ Reading Proficiency, *ATE*, p. 613
____ Enrichment, *ATE*, pp. 616, 620
____ Visual Learning, *ATE*, p. 618

After Reading

Review and Extend
Use the following materials to review and extend the lesson:
____ After Reading, *SE/ATE*, p. 621
____ Use Reading Strategies: Make Connections, *Meeting the Standards Unit 7*, p. 26
____ End Marks, *Exceeding the Standards: Grammar & Style,* pp. 156–158

Assess

Administer the following assessment tool(s):

_____ Selection Quiz, *Meeting the Standards Unit 7*, p. 27

_____ Lesson Test, *Assessment Guide*, pp. 197–199

Technology Tools

Enhance the lesson with interactive activities offered in these technology supplements:

- EMC Launchpad
- Annotated Teacher's Edition on CD
- Interactive Student Text on CD
- *ExamView*® Assessment Suite on CD
- Visual Teaching Package
- ETS Online Criterion-Based Essay Grader (Grades 9–12)
- EMC Audio Library
- EMC E-Library
- **mirrorsandwindows.com**

LESSON PLAN

Name: _____ Date: _____

Grammar & Style Workshop: Verbals: Participles, Gerunds, and Infinitives, p. 622

A Christmas Carol: Scrooge and Marley, Act 1 / *from* **What Jane Austen Ate and Charles Dickens Knew**, p. 623

Directed Reading
- **Reading Level:** Challenging
- **Difficulty Consideration:** Vocabulary and setting
- **Ease Factor:** Familiar, interesting story

Pacing
- **Regular Schedule:** 3 days
- **Block Schedule:** 1.5 days

Objectives
Studying this lesson will enable students to
- use reading skills such as drawing conclusions
- define plot and recognize the conflict that drives the plot
- describe the literary accomplishments of Israel Horovitz
- appreciate a play based on a classic story by Charles Dickens

---

Before Reading

Teach the Workshop(s)
Select from the following materials to teach the workshop(s):
_____ Grammar & Style: Verbals: Participles, Gerunds, and Infinitives, *SE/ATE*, p. 622
_____ Language Arts Handbook Section 3.11, Phrases, *SE/ATE*, pp. 866–867
_____ Verbals, *Exceeding the Standards: Grammar & Style*, pp. 72–74
_____ Verbal Phrases, *Exceeding the Standards: Grammar & Style*, pp. 137–139

Preview and Motivate
Choose from the following materials to preview the lesson and motivate your students:
_____ Before Reading, *SE/ATE*, p. 623
_____ Preview Vocabulary, *Meeting the Standards Unit 7*, p. 28
_____ Vocabulary: Literary Neologisms, *Meeting the Standards Unit 7*, p. 29

During Reading

Teach the Selection(s)
Choose from the following resources to teach the selection(s):
_____ During Reading, *SE/ATE*, pp. 624–641
_____ History Connection: Industry and Reform, *SE/ATE*, p. 634
_____ Informational Text Connection: from "What Jane Austen Ate and Charles Dickens Knew," *SE/ATE*, pp. 642–643
_____ Vocabulary Skills: Extend Vocabulary, *ATE*, p. 626
_____ Grammar Skills: Parallelism, *ATE*, p. 628
_____ Writing Skills: Review, *ATE*, p. 631
_____ Reading Skills: Monitor Comprehension, *ATE*, p. 633
_____ Writing Skills: Character Sketch, *ATE*, p. 635
_____ Grammar Skills: Predicate Adjectives, *ATE*, p. 636
_____ Reading Skills: Compare and Contrast, *ATE*, pp. 637, 639

_____ Speaking & Listening Skills: Panel Discussion, *ATE*, p. 641
_____ Analyze Literature: Asides, *Meeting the Standards Unit 7*, p. 30
_____ Literary Connection: Dynamic Character and Transformation, *Meeting the Standards Unit 7*, p. 31

Differentiate Instruction
Consider the following alternative teaching options to differentiate instruction:
_____ Reading Proficiency, *ATE*, pp. 625, 627, 632, 643
_____ English Language Learning, *ATE*, pp. 627, 632, 643
_____ Visual Learning, *ATE*, p. 629
_____ Auditory Learning, *ATE*, p. 630
_____ Enrichment, *ATE*, pp. 634, 640
_____ Kinesthetic Learning, *ATE*, p. 638
_____ Historical Context Project: Wealth and Poverty in Victorian England, *Differentiated Instruction for Advanced Students*, pp. 41–42

After Reading

Review and Extend
Use the following materials to review and extend the lesson:
_____ After Reading, *SE/ATE*, pp. 641, 644
_____ Text-to-Text Connection, *Meeting the Standards Unit 7*, p. 32
_____ Collaborative Learning: Analyze the Story, *Exceeding the Standards: Extension Activities*, p. 19

Assess
Administer the following assessment tool(s):
_____ Selection Quiz, *Meeting the Standards Unit 7*, p. 33
_____ Lesson Test, *Assessment Guide*, pp. 200–202

Technology Tools
Enhance the lesson with interactive activities offered in these technology supplements:
- EMC Launchpad
- Annotated Teacher's Edition on CD
- Interactive Student Text on CD
- Exam*View*® Assessment Suite on CD
- Visual Teaching Package
- ETS Online Criterion-Based Essay Grader (Grades 9–12)
- EMC Audio Library
- EMC E-Library
- **mirrorsandwindows.com**

Name: _____ Date: _____

M   T   W   Th   F

A Christmas Carol: Scrooge and Marley, Act 2 / *from* A Christmas Carol, p. 645

Vocabulary & Spelling Workshop: Using Dictionaries and Thesauruses, p. 668

Directed Reading
- **Reading Level:** Challenging
- **Difficulty Consideration:** Vocabulary and setting
- **Ease Factor:** Familiar, interesting story

Pacing
- **Regular Schedule:** 3 days
- **Block Schedule:** 1.5 days

Objectives
Studying this lesson will enable students to
- use reading skills such as drawing conclusions
- define plot and recognize the conflict that drives the plot
- describe the literary accomplishments of Israel Horovitz
- appreciate a play based on a classic story by Charles Dickens

---

Before Reading

Preview and Motivate
Choose from the following materials to preview the lesson and motivate your students:
____   Before Reading, *SE/ATE*, p. 645
____   Build Background, *Meeting the Standards Unit 7*, p. 34

During Reading

Teach the Selection(s)
Choose from the following resources to teach the selection(s):
____   During Reading, *SE/ATE*, pp. 645–664
____   Primary Source Connection: from *A Christmas Carol*, *SE/ATE*, pp. 665–666
____   Reading Skills: Activate Prior Knowledge, *ATE*, p. 646
____   Grammar Skills: Collective Nouns, *ATE*, p. 647
____   Writing Skills: Assess Length, *ATE*, p. 651
____   Research Skills: Graphic Organizers, *ATE*, p. 653
____   Grammar Skills: Compound Subjects, *ATE*, p. 655
____   Speaking & Listening Skills: Nonverbal Communication, *ATE*, p. 657
____   Reading Skills: Compare and Contrast, *ATE*, p. 659
____   Writing Skills: Main Idea and Supporting Details, *ATE*, p. 661
____   Grammar Skills: Misplaced Modifiers, *ATE*, p. 662
____   Speaking & Listening Skills: Active Listening, *ATE*, p. 663
____   Reading Skills: Identify Cause and Effect, *ATE*, p. 665
____   Critical Thinking: Make Judgments, *Meeting the Standards Unit 7*, pp. 35–38

Differentiate Instruction

Consider the following alternative teaching options to differentiate instruction:

____ Reading Proficiency, *ATE*, pp. 648, 654, 658

____ English Language Learning, *ATE*, pp. 649, 660

____ Visual and Auditory Learning, *ATE*, p. 650

____ Kinesthetic Learning, *ATE*, p. 652

____ Enrichment, *ATE*, pp. 656, 664

____ Visual Learning, *ATE*, p. 666

____ Kinesthetic and Visual Learning, *ATE*, p. 666

After Reading

Review and Extend

Use the following materials to review and extend the lesson:

____ After Reading, *SE/ATE*, pp. 664, 667

____ Analyze Literature: Theme, *Meeting the Standards Unit 7*, p. 39

____ Text-to-Text Connection, *Meeting the Standards Unit 7*, p. 40

____ Editing for Capitalization Errors, *Exceeding the Standards: Grammar & Style*, pp. 173–175

Teach the Workshop(s)

Select from the following materials to teach the workshop(s):

____ Vocabulary & Spelling: Using Dictionaries and Thesauruses, *SE/ATE*, p. 668

____ Language Arts Handbook Section 2.3, Using a Dictionary, *SE/ATE*, p. 841

____ Using Dictionaries and Thesauruses, *Exceeding the Standards: Vocabulary & Style*, pp. 64–65

____ Choosing the Right Definition, *Exceeding the Standards: Vocabulary & Style*, pp. 66–67

Assess

Administer the following assessment tool(s):

____ Selection Quiz, *Meeting the Standards Unit 7*, pp. 41–42

____ Lesson Test, *Assessment Guide*, pp. 203–205

Technology Tools

Enhance the lesson with interactive activities offered in these technology supplements:

- EMC Launchpad
- Annotated Teacher's Edition on CD
- Interactive Student Text on CD
- Exam*View*® Assessment Suite on CD
- Visual Teaching Package
- ETS Online Criterion-Based Essay Grader (Grades 9–12)
- EMC Audio Library
- EMC E-Library
- **mirrorsandwindows.com**

LESSON PLAN

Name: _____ Date: _____

Let Me Hear You Whisper / *from* Going Ape Over Language, p. 669

Directed Reading
- **Reading Level:** Challenging
- **Difficulty Consideration:** Vocabulary, length, and topic
- **Ease Factor:** Suspense

Pacing
- **Regular Schedule:** 3 days
- **Block Schedule:** 1.5 days

Objectives
Studying this lesson will enable students to
- use reading skills such as distinguishing between major and minor details
- define dialogue and recognize its effects in the selection
- describe the work of Paul Zindel and explain how his early interests may have affected his writing
- appreciate a story about a woman and a dolphin overcoming challenges

Before Reading

Preview and Motivate
Choose from the following materials to preview the lesson and motivate your students:
____   Before Reading, *SE/ATE*, p. 669
____   Build Background: Animal Connection, *Meeting the Standards Unit 7*, p. 43
____   Build Background: Do Online Research, *Meeting the Standards Unit 7*, p. 44

During Reading

Teach the Selection(s)
Choose from the following resources to teach the selection(s):
____   During Reading, *SE/ATE*, pp. 670–682
____   Informational Text Connection: from "Going Ape Over Language," *SE/ATE*, pp. 683–685
____   Reading Skills: Draw Conclusions, *ATE*, p. 672
____   Speaking & Listening Skills: Dramatic Effect, *ATE*, p. 674
____   Grammar Skills: Ellipses, *ATE*, p. 675
____   Reading Skills: Take Notes, *ATE*, p. 677
____   Writing Skills: Dialogue, *ATE*, p. 679
____   Vocabulary Skills: Affixes, *ATE*, p. 681
____   Research Skills: Internet Research, *ATE*, p. 685
____   Use Reading Strategies: Make Inferences, *Meeting the Standards Unit 7*, p. 45

Differentiate Instruction
Consider the following alternative teaching options to differentiate instruction:
____   Reading Proficiency, *ATE*, pp. 671, 678, 684
____   English Language Learning, *ATE*, pp. 673, 684
____   Enrichment, *ATE*, pp. 673, 676, 680
____   Auditory and Kinesthetic Learning, *ATE*, p. 678
____   Communication Analysis: Animal Language, *Differentiated Instruction for Advanced Students*, p. 43

After Reading

Review and Extend

Use the following materials to review and extend the lesson:

_____ After Reading, *SE/ATE*, pp. 682, 686

_____ Text-to-Text Connection, *Meeting the Standards Unit 7*, p. 46

_____ Debate, *Meeting the Standards Unit 7*, p. 47

_____ Critical Literacy: Perform Reader's Theater, *Exceeding the Standards: Extension Activities*, pp. 20–21

_____ Narrative Writing: Write Dialogue, *Exceeding the Standards: Writing*, pp. 47–55

Assess

Administer the following assessment tool(s):

_____ Selection Quiz, *Meeting the Standards Unit 7*, p. 48

_____ Lesson Test, *Assessment Guide*, pp. 206–208

Technology Tools

Enhance the lesson with interactive activities offered in these technology supplements:

- EMC Launchpad
- Annotated Teacher's Edition on CD
- Interactive Student Text on CD
- Exam*View*® Assessment Suite on CD
- Visual Teaching Package
- ETS Online Criterion-Based Essay Grader (Grades 9–12)
- EMC Audio Library
- EMC E-Library
- **mirrorsandwindows.com**

Name: _____ Date: _____

St. Crispian's Day Speech / The Charge of the Light Brigade, p. 687

Grammar & Style Workshop: Punctuation: Dashes, Semicolons, and Colons, p. 693

Directed Reading

"St. Crispian's Day Speech"
- **Reading Level:** Easy
- **Difficulty Consideration:** Subject matter
- **Ease Factor:** Straightforward sentence structure

"The Charge of the Light Brigade"
- **Reading Level:** Challenging
- **Difficulty Consideration:** Sentence structure, subject matter
- **Ease Factor:** Repetition

Pacing
- **Regular Schedule:** 2 days
- **Block Schedule:** 1 day

Objectives

Studying this lesson will enable students to
- compare literary selections of different genres
- use reading skills such as drawing conclusions and making connections
- define diction and compare its effects in two literary works
- recognize some literary accomplishments of William Shakespeare and Alfred, Lord Tennyson
- recognize techniques leaders use to inspire soldiers before battle

---

Before Reading

Preview and Motivate

Choose from the following materials to preview the lesson and motivate your students:

____   Before Reading, *SE/ATE*, p. 687

____   Build Background, Set Purpose, Practice Vocabulary, *Meeting the Standards Unit 7*, pp. 49–50

During Reading

Teach the Selection(s)

Choose from the following resources to teach the selection(s):

____   During Reading, *SE/ATE*, pp. 688–691

____   Cultural Connection: Crimean War, *SE/ATE*, p. 691

____   Compare Literature: Diction, *Meeting the Standards Unit 7*, p. 51

Differentiate Instruction

Consider the following alternative teaching options to differentiate instruction:

____   Reading Proficiency, *ATE*, p. 689

____   English Language Learning, *ATE*, pp. 689, 691

____   Enrichment, *ATE*, p. 691

____   Literature Comparison: Wartime Speeches, *Differentiated Instruction for Advanced Students*, p. 44

After Reading

Review and Extend

Use the following materials to review and extend the lesson:

____ After Reading, *SE/ATE*, pp. 689, 692
____ Compare Literature: Diction (continued), *Meeting the Standards Unit 7*, p. 52
____ Compare Literature: Poetic Devices, *Meeting the Standards Unit 7*, p. 53
____ Use Reading Strategies: Make Connections, *Meeting the Standards Unit 7*, p. 54
____ What Do You Think? *Meeting the Standards Unit 7*, p. 58

Teach the Workshop(s)

Select from the following materials to teach the workshop(s):

____ Grammar & Style: Punctuation: Dashes, Semicolons, and Colons, *SE/ATE*, p. 693
____ Language Arts Handbook Section 3.15, Punctuation, *SE/ATE*, pp. 876–881
____ Commas, *Exceeding the Standards: Grammar & Style*, pp. 159–162
____ Semicolons, *Exceeding the Standards: Grammar & Style*, pp. 163–164
____ Hyphens and Dashes, *Exceeding the Standards: Grammar & Style*, pp. 171–172

Assess

Administer the following assessment tool(s):

____ Selection Quiz: Focus on "St. Crispian's Day Speech," *Meeting the Standards Unit 7*, pp. 55–56
____ Selection Quiz: Focus on "The Charge of the Light Brigade," *Meeting the Standards Unit 7*, p. 57
____ Lesson Test, *Assessment Guide*, pp. 209–210

Technology Tools

Enhance the lesson with interactive activities offered in these technology supplements:

- EMC Launchpad
- Annotated Teacher's Edition on CD
- Interactive Student Text on CD
- Exam*View*® Assessment Suite on CD
- Visual Teaching Package
- ETS Online Criterion-Based Essay Grader (Grades 9–12)
- EMC Audio Library
- EMC E-Library
- **mirrorsandwindows.com**

Name: _____ Date: _____

The Monsters Are Due on Maple Street, p. 694

Independent Reading
- **Reading Level:** Challenging
- **Difficulty Consideration:** Length, vocabulary, and science concepts
- **Ease Factor:** Exciting plot

Pacing
- **Regular Schedule:** 2 days
- **Block Schedule:** 1 day

Objectives
Studying this lesson will enable students to
- read with developing fluency
- read silently with comprehension for a sustained period of time

Before Reading

Preview and Motivate
Choose from the following materials to preview the lesson and motivate your students:
____ Before Reading, *SE/ATE*, p. 694
____ Practice Vocabulary, *Meeting the Standards Unit 7*, p. 59

During Reading

Teach the Selection(s)
Choose from the following resources to teach the selection(s):
____ During Reading, *SE/ATE*, pp. 694–708
____ Speaking & Listening Skills: Inflection, *ATE*, p. 697
____ Grammar Skills: Sentence Fragments, *ATE*, p. 698
____ Research Skills: Evaluate Sources, *ATE*, p. 699
____ Speaking & Listening Skills: Dramatic Reading, *ATE*, p. 701
____ Vocabulary Skills: Idioms, *ATE*, p. 703
____ Grammar Skills: Apostrophes, *ATE*, p. 705
____ Reading Skills: Compare and Contrast, *ATE*, p. 707
____ Analyze Dialogue, *Meeting the Standards Unit 7*, pp. 60–61

Differentiate Instruction
Consider the following alternative teaching options to differentiate instruction:
____ Reading Proficiency, *ATE*, pp. 696, 702, 704
____ Auditory Learning, *ATE*, p. 702
____ English Language Learning, *ATE*, p. 704
____ Auditory and Kinesthetic Learning, *ATE*, p. 706
____ Enrichment, *ATE*, p. 708
____ Media Study: Mood and Tone in Visual Media, *Differentiated Instruction for Advanced Students*, p. 45
____ Reading Strategies and Skills Practice: Use Text Organization, *Differentiated Instruction for Developing Readers*, pp. 49–81

After Reading

Review and Extend

Use the following materials to review and extend the lesson:

_____ After Reading, *SE/ATE*, p. 708

_____ Analyze Cause and Effect, *Meeting the Standards Unit 7*, p. 62

_____ Analyze Stage Directions, *Meeting the Standards Unit 7*, pp. 63–64

_____ Describe and Critique: Drama, *Meeting the Standards Unit 7*, pp. 65–68

Assess

Administer the following assessment tool(s):

_____ Lesson Test, *Assessment Guide*, pp. 212–214

Technology Tools

Enhance the lesson with interactive activities offered in these technology supplements:

- EMC Launchpad
- Annotated Teacher's Edition on CD
- Interactive Student Text on CD
- Exam*View*® Assessment Suite on CD
- Visual Teaching Package
- ETS Online Criterion-Based Essay Grader (Grades 9–12)
- EMC Audio Library
- EMC E-Library
- **mirrorsandwindows.com**

LESSON PLAN

Name: _____ Date: _____

                M   T   W   Th   F

Writing Workshop: Persuasive Writing—Persuasive Essay, p. 710

Pacing
- **Regular Schedule:** 3 days
- **Block Schedule:** 1.5 days

Objectives
Participating in this lesson will help enable students to
- write a persuasive essay that has an effective introduction
- write a persuasive essay that has a clear thesis statement
- write a persuasive essay that has a clear organizational pattern
- write a persuasive essay that has evidence that supports the thesis
- write a persuasive essay that has a conclusion that restates the thesis and adds insight

---

Teach the Workshop
Select from the following resources to teach the workshop:

_____ Writing Workshop: Persuasive Writing—Persuasive Essay, *SE/ATE*, pp. 710–715
_____ Reading Skills: Determine Importance of Details, *ATE*, p. 711
_____ Writing Skills: Rhetorical Devices, *ATE*, p. 713
_____ Vocabulary Skills: Denotation and Connotation, *ATE*, p. 715
_____ Language Arts Handbook Section 4.1, The Writing Process, *SE/ATE*, pp. 888–897
_____ Language Arts Handbook Section 4.2, Modes and Purposes of Writing, *SE/ATE*, p. 897

Differentiate Instruction
Consider the following alternative teaching options to differentiate instruction:

_____ Enrichment, *ATE*, p. 712
_____ Auditory Learning, *ATE*, p. 714

Review and Extend
Use the following materials to review and extend the lesson:

_____ Narrative Writing: Write Dialogue, *Exceeding the Standards: Writing*, pp. 47–55

Technology Tools
Enhance the lesson with interactive activities offered in these technology supplements:

- EMC Launchpad
- Annotated Teacher's Edition on CD
- Interactive Student Text on CD
- Exam*View*® Assessment Suite on CD
- Visual Teaching Package
- ETS Online Criterion-Based Essay Grader (Grades 9–12)
- EMC Audio Library
- EMC E-Library
- **mirrorsandwindows.com**

Name: _____ Date: _____

M   T   W   Th   F

Speaking & Listening Workshop: Giving and Actively Listening to Persuasive Presentations, p. 716

Pacing
- **Regular Schedule:** 2 days
- **Block Schedule:** 1 day

Objectives
Participating in this lesson will help enable students to
- deliver persuasive presentations that open and close strongly
- deliver persuasive presentations that promote a solid viewpoint
- deliver persuasive presentations that use valid arguments
- deliver persuasive presentations that present ideas clearly
- deliver persuasive presentations that employ persuasive techniques convincingly
- deliver persuasive presentations that incorporate effective pacing, volume, and nonverbal expression

Teach the Workshop
Select from the following resources to teach the workshop:
_____ Speaking & Listening Workshop: Giving and Actively Listening to Persuasive Presentations, *SE/ATE*, pp. 716–717
_____ Language Arts Handbook Section 7.1, Verbal and Nonverbal Communication, *SE/ATE*, p. 912
_____ Language Arts Handbook Section 7.2, Listening Skills, *SE/ATE*, pp. 913–914
_____ Language Arts Handbook Section 7.3, Collaborative Learning and Communication, *SE/ATE*, pp. 914–915
_____ Language Arts Handbook Section 7.6, Public Speaking, *SE/ATE*, pp. 916–917

Differentiate Instruction
Consider the following alternative teaching options to differentiate instruction:
_____ Reading Proficiency, *ATE*, p. 717

Review and Extend
Use the following materials to review and extend the lesson:
_____ Giving and Actively Listening to Research Presentations, *Exceeding the Standards: Speaking & Listening*, pp. 19–22

Technology Tools
Enhance the lesson with interactive activities offered in these technology supplements:
- EMC Launchpad
- Annotated Teacher's Edition on CD
- Interactive Student Text on CD
- Exam*View*® Assessment Suite on CD
- Visual Teaching Package
- ETS Online Criterion-Based Essay Grader (Grades 9–12)
- EMC Audio Library
- EMC E-Library
- **mirrorsandwindows.com**

Name: _____ Date: _____

M   T   W   Th   F

Test Practice Workshop, p. 718

Pacing
- **Regular Schedule:** 1 day
- **Block Schedule:** 0.5 day

Objectives
Participating in this lesson will help enable students to
- write a persuasive essay based on a timed writing prompt

- answer standardized test questions that demonstrate revising and editing skills
- answer standardized questions that demonstrate the ability to make inferences from a reading

---

Teach the Workshop
Select from the following resources to teach the workshop:
____   Writing Skills: Persuasive Essay, *SE/ATE*, p. 718
____   Revising and Editing Skills, *SE/ATE*, p. 719
____   Reading Skills, *SE/ATE*, pp. 720–721
____   Test-Taking Skills: Choose the Best Answer, *ATE*, p. 721
____   Language Arts Handbook Section 8.1, Preparing for Tests, *SE/ATE*, p. 921
____   Language Arts Handbook Section 8.2, Strategies for Taking Standardized Tests, *SE/ATE*, pp. 921–922
____   Language Arts Handbook Section 8.3, Answering Objective Questions, *SE/ATE*, p. 922
____   Language Arts Handbook Section 8.4, Answering Multiple-Choice Questions, *SE/ATE*, p. 922
____   Language Arts Handbook Section 8.5, Answering Reading Comprehension Questions, *SE/ATE*, p. 923
____   Language Arts Handbook Section 8.8, Answering Constructed-Response Questions, *SE/ATE*, pp. 923–924
____   Language Arts Handbook Section 8.9, Answering Essay Questions, *SE/ATE*, pp. 924–925
____   Test-Taking Skills and Strategies, *Exceeding the Standards: Test Practice*, pp. 1–4

Differentiate Instruction
Consider the following alternative teaching options to differentiate instruction:
____   English Language Learning, *ATE*, p. 720

Review and Extend
Use the following materials to review and extend the lesson:
____   Drama Study Guide: Practice Test, *Meeting the Standards Unit 7*, pp. 11–16
____   ACT Practice Test, *Exceeding the Standards: Test Practice*, pp. 16–19

Technology Tools
Enhance the lesson with interactive activities offered in these technology supplements:
- EMC Launchpad
- Annotated Teacher's Edition on CD
- Interactive Student Text on CD
- Exam*View*® Assessment Suite on CD
- Visual Teaching Package
- ETS Online Criterion-Based Essay Grader (Grades 9–12)
- EMC Audio Library
- EMC E-Library
- **mirrorsandwindows.com**

Name: _____ Date: _____

M   T   W   Th   F

Unit 8 Folk Literature Opener, p. 722

Pacing
- **Regular Schedule:** 1 day
- **Block Schedule:** 0.5 day

Objectives
Studying this lesson will enable students to
- connect a theme expressed in a selection to their own lives
- identify common forms and elements of literature from the oral tradition

Plan the Unit

Use the following resources to plan instruction for this unit:
_____ Unit 8 Visual Planning Guide: Unit-Based Resources, *ATE*, pp. 722A–722B
_____ Unit 8 Visual Planning Guide: Lesson-by-Lesson Resources, *ATE*, pp. 722C–722E
_____ Unit 8 Scope & Sequence Guide, *ATE*, pp. 722E–722H
_____ Unit 8 Building Vocabulary, *ATE*, pp. 722I–722J
_____ Launch the Unit, *ATE*, p. 722

Teach the Unit Opener

Choose from the following resources to teach the unit opener:
_____ Unit 8 Overview, *SE/ATE*, pp. 722–723
_____ Introduction to Folk Literature, *SE/ATE*, pp. 724–725
_____ Folk Literature Study Guide: Introduction, *Meeting the Standards Unit 8*, p. 1
_____ Folk Literature Study Guide: Understanding Introduction to Folk Literature and Applying Folk Literature to the Selections, *Meeting the Standards Unit 8*, pp. 2–6
_____ Folk Literature Study Guide: Reviewing Character and Theme and Applying Character and Theme to the Selections, *Meeting the Standards Unit 8*, pp. 7–8
_____ Folk Literature Study Guide: Reviewing Imagery and Figurative Language and Applying Imagery and Figurative Language to the Selections, *Meeting the Standards Unit 8*, pp. 9–10
_____ Folk Literature Study Guide: Master Vocabulary List, *Meeting the Standards Unit 8*, p. 17

Differentiate Instruction

Consider the following alternative teaching options to differentiate instruction:
_____ English Language Learning, *ATE*, p. 725
_____ Enrichment, *ATE*, p. 725

Extend the Unit

Choose from the following resources to extend the unit:
_____ For Your Reading List, *SE/ATE*, p. 805
_____ Unit 8, *Exceeding the Standards: Grammar & Style*, pp. 186–200
_____ Read and Discuss Folklore, Superstition, and Science, *Exceeding the Standards: Literature & Reading*, pp. 21–23.
_____ Lifelong Learning: Setting Goals: Part 1, *Exceeding the Standards: Special Topics*, pp. 31–32
_____ Career Skills Development: Conducting an Internet Job Search, *Exceeding the Standards: Special Topics*, pp. 33–35
_____ Unit 8, *Exceeding the Standards: Vocabulary & Spelling*, pp. 71–78

Assess

Administer the following assessment tool(s):

____ Formative Surveys 1 and 2, *Assessment Guide*, pp. 3–20

____ Reading Fluency Assessments, Passages 1 and 2, *Assessment Guide*, pp. 307–308

____ Unit 8 Exam, *Assessment Guide*, pp. 281–284

Technology Tools

Enhance the lesson with interactive activities offered in these technology supplements:

- EMC Launchpad
- Annotated Teacher's Edition on CD
- Interactive Student Text on CD
- Exam*View*® Assessment Suite on CD
- Visual Teaching Package
- ETS Online Criterion-Based Essay Grader (Grades 9–12)
- EMC Audio Library
- EMC E-Library
- **mirrorsandwindows.com**

Name: _____ Date: _____

Persephone and Demeter, p. 727

Guided Reading: Reading Model
- **Reading Level:** Moderate
- **Difficulty Consideration:** Vocabulary
- **Ease Factor:** Length

Pacing
- **Regular Schedule:** 2 days
- **Block Schedule:** 1 day

Objectives
Studying this lesson will enable students to
- use reading skills such as monitoring comprehension

- define myth and recognize the elements of the selection that identify it as a myth
- define the literary accomplishments of Ingri d'Aulaire and Edgar Parin d'Aulaire and explain the role they played in exposing English-speaking readers to myths and folklore of various cultures
- appreciate a myth about the origin of the seasons

Before Reading

Preview and Motivate

Choose from the following materials to preview the lesson and motivate your students:

_____ Folk Literature Reading Model, *SE/ATE*, p. 726
_____ Before Reading, *SE/ATE*, p. 727
_____ How to Read Folk Literature, *Meeting the Standards Unit 8*, p. 19
_____ Apply the Model, *Meeting the Standards Unit 8*, p. 20
_____ Mythology Connection, *Meeting the Standards Unit 8*, p. 21
_____ Build Background, *Meeting the Standards Unit 8*, pp. 22–23

During Reading

Teach the Selection(s)

Choose from the following resources to teach the selection(s):

_____ During Reading, *SE/ATE*, pp. 728–731
_____ Reading Skills: Compare and Contrast, *ATE*, p. 731
_____ Use Reading Strategies: Make Predictions, *Meeting the Standards Unit 8*, p. 24

Differentiate Instruction

Consider the following alternative teaching options to differentiate instruction:

_____ English Language Learning, *ATE*, p. 729
_____ Reading Proficiency, *ATE*, p. 729
_____ Enrichment, *ATE*, p. 730
_____ Auditory Learning, *ATE*, p. 730
_____ Reading Strategies and Skills Practice: Make Connections, *Differentiated Instruction for Developing Readers*, pp. 52–53
_____ Monitor Comprehension, *Differentiated Instruction for English Language Learners*, pp. 175–183

After Reading

Review and Extend

Use the following materials to review and extend the lesson:

____ After Reading, *SE/ATE*, p.732

____ Vocabulary Building: Mad Lib, *Meeting the Standards Unit 8*, pp. 25–26

____ Lifelong Learning: Find a Myth, *Exceeding the Standards: Extension Activities*, pp. 22–23

Assess

Administer the following assessment tool(s):

____ Selection Quiz, *Meeting the Standards Unit 8*, p. 27

____ Lesson Test, *Assessment Guide*, pp. 215–217

Technology Tools

Enhance the lesson with interactive activities offered in these technology supplements:

- EMC Launchpad
- Annotated Teacher's Edition on CD
- Interactive Student Text on CD
- Exam*View*® Assessment Suite on CD
- Visual Teaching Package
- ETS Online Criterion-Based Essay Grader (Grades 9–12)
- EMC Audio Library
- EMC E-Library
- **mirrorsandwindows.com**

Name: _____ Date: _____

M T W Th F

Eshu, p. 733

Guided Reading: Reading Model
- **Reading Level:** Moderate
- **Difficulty Consideration:** Context and confusing ending
- **Ease Factor:** Dialogue

Pacing
- **Regular Schedule:** 1 day
- **Block Schedule:** 0.5 day

Objectives
Studying this lesson will enable students to
- use reading skills such as identifying the main idea
- define folk tale and recognize the selection as an example
- describe Judith Gleason's role in popularizing African folk tales
- appreciate a folk tale featuring a trickster character

Before Reading

Preview and Motivate
Choose from the following materials to preview the lesson and motivate your students:
____ Fiction Reading Model, *SE/ATE*, p. 726
____ Before Reading, *SE/ATE*, p. 733
____ Build Background: Friendship, *Meeting the Standards Unit 8*, pp. 28–29
____ Build Vocabulary, *Meeting the Standards Unit 8*, p. 30

During Reading

Teach the Selection(s)
Choose from the following resources to teach the selection(s):
____ During Reading, *SE/ATE*, pp. 734–736
____ Use Reading Skills: Retell Sequence, *Meeting the Standards Unit 8*, p. 31

Differentiate Instruction
Consider the following alternative teaching options to differentiate instruction:
____ English Language Learning, *ATE*, p. 735
____ Reading Proficiency, *ATE*, p. 735
____ Enrichment, *ATE*, p. 736
____ Auditory and Kinesthetic Learning, *ATE*, p. 736
____ Cultural Connection Analysis: The Yoruban People, *Differentiated Instruction for Advanced Students*, p. 46

After Reading

Review and Extend
Use the following materials to review and extend the lesson:
____ After Reading, *SE/ATE*, p.737
____ Analyze Literature: Describe and Critique, *Meeting the Standards Unit 8*, p. 32

Assess

Administer the following assessment tool(s):

_____ Selection Quiz, *Meeting the Standards Unit 1*, p. 33

_____ Lesson Test, *Assessment Guide*, pp. 218–220

Technology Tools

Enhance the lesson with interactive activities offered in these technology supplements:

- EMC Launchpad
- Annotated Teacher's Edition on CD
- Interactive Student Text on CD
- Exam*View*® Assessment Suite on CD
- Visual Teaching Package
- ETS Online Criterion-Based Essay Grader (Grades 9–12)
- EMC Audio Library
- EMC E-Library
- **mirrorsandwindows.com**

Name: _____ Date: _____

M   T   W   Th   F

The Secret Name of Ra / *from* Akhenaton's Hymn to the Sun, p. 738
Vocabulary & Spelling Workshop: Homographs, Homophones, and Homonyms, p. 746

Directed Reading
- **Reading Level:** Moderate
- **Difficulty Consideration:** Vocabulary
- **Ease Factor:** Length

Pacing
- **Regular Schedule:** 3 days
- **Block Schedule:** 1.5 days

Objectives
Studying this lesson will enable students to
- use reading skills such as analyzing cause and effect
- define motivation and recognize how this literary technique is used in connection with characters
- describe literary accomplishments of Geraldine Harris
- appreciate an Egyptian myth about a power struggle between the gods

---

Before Reading

Preview and Motivate
Choose from the following materials to preview the lesson and motivate your students:
_____ Before Reading, *SE/ATE*, p. 738
_____ Preview Vocabulary, *Meeting the Standards Unit 8*, p. 34
_____ Collaborative Learning: History Research Project, *Meeting the Standards Unit 8*, p. 35

During Reading

Teach the Selection(s)
Choose from the following resources to teach the selection(s):
_____ During Reading, *SE/ATE*, pp. 739–742
_____ History Connection: Ancient Egypt, *SE/ATE*, p. 741
_____ Literature Connection: from "Akhenaton's Hymn to the Sun," *SE/ATE*, pp. 743–744
_____ Writing Skills: Summarizing, *ATE*, p. 741
_____ Use Reading Skills: Clarify, *Meeting the Standards Unit 8*, p. 36

Differentiate Instruction
Consider the following alternative teaching options to differentiate instruction:
_____ Enrichment, *ATE*, p. 740
_____ English Language Learning, *ATE*, pp. 740, 744
_____ Reading Proficiency, *ATE*, pp. 742, 744
_____ Visual Learning, *ATE*, p. 742
_____ Analyze Cause and Effect, *Differentiated Instruction for English Language Learners*, p. 46

After Reading

Review and Extend

Use the following materials to review and extend the lesson:

_____ After Reading, *SE/ATE*, pp. 742, 745

_____ Make Connections, *Meeting the Standards Unit 8*, p. 37

Teach the Workshop(s)

Select from the following materials to teach the workshop(s):

_____ Vocabulary & Spelling: Homographs, Homophones, and Homonyms, *SE/ATE*, p. 746

_____ Language Arts Handbook Section 2.5, Understanding Multiple Meanings, *SE/ATE*, p. 842

_____ Language Arts Handbook Section 2.7, Spelling, *SE/ATE*, pp. 843–851

_____ Homographs, Homophones, and Homonyms, *Exceeding the Standards: Vocabulary & Spelling*, pp. 58–59

_____ More about Homographs, Homophones, and Homonyms, *Exceeding the Standards: Vocabulary & Spelling*, pp. 60–63

Assess

Administer the following assessment tool(s):

_____ Selection Quiz, *Meeting the Standards Unit 1*, pp. 38–39

_____ Lesson Test, *Assessment Guide*, pp. 221–223

Technology Tools

Enhance the lesson with interactive activities offered in these technology supplements:

- EMC Launchpad
- Annotated Teacher's Edition on CD
- Interactive Student Text on CD
- Exam*View*® Assessment Suite on CD
- Visual Teaching Package
- ETS Online Criterion-Based Essay Grader (Grades 9–12)
- EMC Audio Library
- EMC E-Library
- **mirrorsandwindows.com**

LESSON PLAN

Tsali of the Cherokees / Moving West: A Native American Perspective, p. 747

Directed Reading
- **Reading Level:** Moderate
- **Difficulty Consideration:** Vocabulary
- **Ease Factor:** Sympathetic narrator and plot

Pacing
- **Regular Schedule:** 3 days
- **Block Schedule:** 1.5 days

Objectives
Studying this lesson will enable students to
- use reading skills such as identifying an author's purpose
- define motivation and analyze its use in the selection
- describe the work of Alice Lee Marriott and Christine Graf, and recognize how their backgrounds influence their writing
- compare an oral history to a magazine article
- observe ways in which people respond to pressures that test their limits

Before Reading

Preview and Motivate

Choose from the following materials to preview the lesson and motivate your students:
____   Before Reading, *SE/ATE*, p. 747
____   Activate Prior Knowledge, *Meeting the Standards Unit 8*, p. 40

During Reading

Teach the Selection(s)

Choose from the following resources to teach the selection(s):
____   During Reading, *SE/ATE*, pp. 748–754
____   Social Studies Connection: Indian Removal, *SE/ATE*, p. 751
____   Informational Text Connection: "Moving West: A Native American Perspective," *SE/ATE*, p. 755
____   Reading Skills: Take Notes, *ATE*, p. 750
____   Vocabulary Skills: Denotation and Connotation, *ATE*, p. 752
____   Grammar Skills: Dangling and Misplaced Modifiers, *ATE*, p. 753
____   Grammar Skills: Phrases, *ATE*, p. 755
____   Build Vocabulary, *Meeting the Standards Unit 8*, p. 41
____   Use Reading Skills: Cause and Effect, *Meeting the Standards Unit 8*, p. 42

Differentiate Instruction

Consider the following alternative teaching options to differentiate instruction:
____   English Language Learning, *ATE*, p. 749
____   Kinesthetic Learners, *ATE*, p. 751
____   Enrichment, *ATE*, p. 754

After Reading

Review and Extend

Use the following materials to review and extend the lesson:

____ After Reading, *SE/ATE*, pp. 754, 756

____ Analyze Literature: Compare and Contrast, *Meeting the Standards Unit 8*, p. 43

____ Wordy Sentences, *Exceeding the Standards: Grammar & Style*, pp. 207–210

Assess

Administer the following assessment tool(s):

____ Selection Quiz, *Meeting the Standards Unit 1,* pp. 44–45

____ Lesson Test, *Assessment Guide*, pp. 224–226

Technology Tools

Enhance the lesson with interactive activities offered in these technology supplements:

- EMC Launchpad
- Annotated Teacher's Edition on CD
- Interactive Student Text on CD
- Exam*View*® Assessment Suite on CD
- Visual Teaching Package
- ETS Online Criterion-Based Essay Grader (Grades 9–12)
- EMC Audio Library
- EMC E-Library
- **mirrorsandwindows.com**

Name: _____ Date: _____

M   T   W   Th   F

We Are All One, p. 757

Grammar & Style Workshop: Misplaced Modifiers, p. 764

Directed Reading
- **Reading Level:** Easy
- **Difficulty Consideration:** Setting
- **Ease Factor:** Manageable segments and dialogue

Pacing
- **Regular Schedule:** 1 day
- **Block Schedule:** 0.5 day

Objectives
Studying this lesson will enable students to
- use reading skills such as determining the sequence of events
- define conflict and recognize conflict in the selection
- describe literary accomplishments of Laurence Yep
- appreciate a Chinese folk tale

Before Reading

Preview and Motivate
Choose from the following materials to preview the lesson and motivate your students:
_____ Before Reading, *SE/ATE*, p. 757
_____ Creative Writing: Vocabulary Preview Paragraph / Vocabulary Building: Negative Prefixes, *Meeting the Standards Unit 8*, p. 46

During Reading

Teach the Selection(s)
Choose from the following resources to teach the selection(s):
_____ During Reading, *SE/ATE*, pp. 757–762
_____ Reading Skills: Identify Text Structure, *ATE*, p. 761
_____ Analyze Literature: Characters, *Meeting the Standards Unit 8*, p. 47

Differentiate Instruction
Consider the following alternative teaching options to differentiate instruction:
_____ Enrichment, *ATE*, pp. 759, 760
_____ Reading Proficiency, *ATE*, pp. 759
_____ Visual Learning, *ATE*, p. 760
_____ English Language Learning, *ATE*, p. 762
_____ Author/Theme Study: Laurence Yep, *Differentiated Instruction for Advanced Students*, p. 47

After Reading

Review and Extend
Use the following materials to review and extend the lesson:
_____ After Reading, *SE/ATE*, p. 763
_____ Use Reading Skills: Sequence of Events, *Meeting the Standards Unit 8*, p. 48

Teach the Workshop(s)

Select from the following materials to teach the workshop(s):

____ Grammar & Style: Misplaced Modifiers, *SE/ATE*, p. 764
____ Language Arts Handbook Section 3.8, Modifiers, *SE/ATE*, p. 842
____ Avoiding Misplaced Modifiers, *Exceeding the Standards: Grammar & Style*, pp. 195–197

Assess

Administer the following assessment tool(s):

____ Selection Quiz, *Meeting the Standards Unit 1,* pp. 49–50
____ Lesson Test, *Assessment Guide*, pp. 227–229

Technology Tools

Enhance the lesson with interactive activities offered in these technology supplements:

- EMC Launchpad
- Annotated Teacher's Edition on CD
- Interactive Student Text on CD
- Exam*View*® Assessment Suite on CD
- Visual Teaching Package

- ETS Online Criterion-Based Essay Grader (Grades 9–12)
- EMC Audio Library
- EMC E-Library
- **mirrorsandwindows.com**

Name: _____ Date: _____

Ant and Grasshopper / The Fox and the Crow / The Lion and the Statue, p. 765

Directed Reading
- **Reading Level:** Easy
- **Difficulty Consideration:** Clarity of morals
- **Ease Factor:** Length

Pacing
- **Regular Schedule:** 1 day
- **Block Schedule:** 0.5 day

Objectives
Studying this lesson will enable students to
- use reading skills such as identifying the author's purpose
- define fable and recognize how the three readings are examples of this genre
- describe the ancient fables credited to a figure named Aesop and recognize their influence on later works of literature
- appreciate entertaining stories of lessons learned

Before Reading

Preview and Motivate
Choose from the following materials to preview the lesson and motivate your students:
_____ Before Reading, *SE/ATE*, p. 765
_____ Build Background, *Meeting the Standards Unit 8*, p. 51

During Reading

Teach the Selection(s)
Choose from the following resources to teach the selection(s):
_____ During Reading, *SE/ATE*, pp. 765–768
_____ Use Reading Skills: Analyze Cause and Effect, *Meeting the Standards Unit 8*, p. 52

Differentiate Instruction
Consider the following alternative teaching options to differentiate instruction:
_____ English Language Learning, *ATE*, p. 767
_____ Enrichment, *ATE*, p. 767
_____ Reading Proficiency, *ATE*, p. 768
_____ Identify Author's Purpose, *Differentiated Instruction for English Language Learners*, pp. 193–199

After Reading

Review and Extend
Use the following materials to review and extend the lesson:
_____ After Reading, *SE/ATE*, p. 769
_____ Find Meaning: Recall, *Meeting the Standards Unit 8*, p. 53
_____ Extend Understanding: Creative Writing, *Meeting the Standards Unit 8*, p. 54
_____ Narrative Writing: Write a Fable, *Exceeding the Standards: Writing*, pp. 56–64

Assess

Administer the following assessment tool(s):

____ Selection Quiz, *Meeting the Standards Unit 1*, p. 55

____ Lesson Test, *Assessment Guide*, pp. 230–232

Technology Tools

Enhance the lesson with interactive activities offered in these technology supplements:

- EMC Launchpad
- Annotated Teacher's Edition on CD
- Interactive Student Text on CD
- Exam*View*® Assessment Suite on CD
- Visual Teaching Package
- ETS Online Criterion-Based Essay Grader (Grades 9–12)
- EMC Audio Library
- EMC E-Library
- **mirrorsandwindows.com**

Name: _____ Date: _____

M   T   W   Th   F

Phaëthon, Son of Apollo, p. 770

Grammar & Style: Dangling Modifiers, p. 776

Directed Reading
- **Reading Level:** Moderate
- **Difficulty Consideration:** Background and names
- **Ease Factor:** Description and suspense

Pacing
- **Regular Schedule:** 2 days
- **Block Schedule:** 1 day

Objectives
Studying this lesson will enable students to
- use reading skills such as drawing conclusions
- define allegory and recognize how it is used in the selection
- describe literary accomplishments of Olivia Coolidge
- appreciate a Greek myth about how pride and foolishness lead to a hero's downfall

---

Before Reading

Preview and Motivate
Choose from the following materials to preview the lesson and motivate your students:
_____   Before Reading, *SE/ATE*, p. 770
_____   Creative Writing, *Meeting the Standards Unit 8*, p. 56

During Reading

Teach the Selection(s)
Choose from the following resources to teach the selection(s):
_____   During Reading, *SE/ATE*, pp. 771–774
_____   Science Connection: Solar Models, *SE/ATE*, p. 773
_____   Grammar Skills: Inverted Sentences, *SE/ATE*, p. 773
_____   Build Vocabulary, *Meeting the Standards Unit 8*, p. 57
_____   Make Connections, *Meeting the Standards Unit 8*, p. 58

Differentiate Instruction
Consider the following alternative teaching options to differentiate instruction:
_____   Reading Proficiency, *ATE*, p. 772
_____   Enrichment, *ATE*, p. 772
_____   English Language Learning, *ATE*, p. 772
_____   Comparison of Myths: Sun Myths Around the World, *Differentiated Instruction for Advanced Students*, p. 48

After Reading

Review and Extend
Use the following materials to review and extend the lesson:
_____   After Reading, *SE/ATE*, p. 775
_____   Evaluating Cause and Effect, *Meeting the Standards Unit 8*, p. 59
_____   Science Connection, *Meeting the Standards Unit 8*, p. 60

Teach the Workshop(s)

Select from the following materials to teach the workshop(s):

____ Grammar & Style: Dangling Modifiers, *SE/ATE*, p. 776

____ Language Arts Handbook Section 3.8, Modifiers, *SE/ATE*, p. 842

____ Avoiding Dangling Modifiers, *Exceeding the Standards: Grammar & Style*, pp. 193–194

Assess

Administer the following assessment tool(s):

____ Selection Quiz, *Meeting the Standards Unit 1*, p. 61

____ Lesson Test, *Assessment Guide*, pp. 233–235

Technology Tools

Enhance the lesson with interactive activities offered in these technology supplements:

- EMC Launchpad
- Annotated Teacher's Edition on CD
- Interactive Student Text on CD
- Exam*View*® Assessment Suite on CD
- Visual Teaching Package
- ETS Online Criterion-Based Essay Grader (Grades 9–12)
- EMC Audio Library
- EMC E-Library
- **mirrorsandwindows.com**

Name: _____ Date: _____

M   T   W   Th   F

The Instruction of Indra / Such Perfection, p. 777

Directed Reading
"The Instruction of Indra"
- **Reading Level:** Challenging
- **Difficulty Consideration:** Setting, concepts, and vocabulary
- **Ease Factor:** None

"Such Perfection"
- **Reading Level:** Moderate
- **Difficulty Consideration:** Cultural and religious background
- **Ease Factor:** Description, simple narrative

Pacing
- **Regular Schedule:** 3 days
- **Block Schedule:** 1.5 days

Objectives
Studying this lesson will enable students to
- compare literary selections of different genres
- use reading skills such as monitoring comprehension
- define symbolism and analyze its use in the selections
- describe literary accomplishments of Joseph Campbell and R. K. Narayan
- appreciate stories about gaining greater wisdom

Before Reading

Preview and Motivate
Choose from the following materials to preview the lesson and motivate your students:
____   Before Reading, *SE/ATE*, p. 777
____   Build Background, Set Purpose, and Practice Vocabulary, *Meeting the Standards Unit 8*, p. 62

During Reading

Teach the Selection(s)
Choose from the following resources to teach the selection(s):
____   During Reading, *SE/ATE*, pp. 778–784
____   Compare Literature: Symbolism, *Meeting the Standards Unit 8*, p. 63

Differentiate Instruction
Consider the following alternative teaching options to differentiate instruction:
____   Visual Learning, *ATE*, p. 779
____   English Language Learning, *ATE*, pp. 780, 784
____   Enrichment, *ATE*, pp. 781, 783
____   Reading Proficiency, *ATE*, pp. 781, 783
____   Reading Strategies and Skills Practice: Set Purpose, *Differentiated Instruction for Developing Readers*, pp. 55–57

After Reading

Review and Extend

Use the following materials to review and extend the lesson:

____ After Reading, *SE/ATE*, pp. 781, 785
____ Compare Literature: Symbolism (continued), *Meeting the Standards Unit 8*, p. 64
____ Compare Literature: Theme, *Meeting the Standards Unit 8*, pp. 65–66
____ Use Reading Strategies: Make Connections, *Meeting the Standards Unit 8*, p. 67
____ What Do You Think? *Meeting the Standards Unit 8*, p. 71

Assess

Administer the following assessment tool(s):

____ Selection Quiz: Focus on "The Instruction of Indra," *Meeting the Standards Unit 1*, pp. 68–69
____ Selection Quiz: Focus on "Such Perfection," *Meeting the Standards Unit 1*, p. 70
____ Lesson Test, *Assessment Guide*, pp. 236–238

Technology Tools

Enhance the lesson with interactive activities offered in these technology supplements:

- EMC Launchpad
- Annotated Teacher's Edition on CD
- Interactive Student Text on CD
- Exam*View*® Assessment Suite on CD
- Visual Teaching Package
- ETS Online Criterion-Based Essay Grader (Grades 9–12)
- EMC Audio Library
- EMC E-Library
- **mirrorsandwindows.com**

Name: _____ Date: _____

M   T   W   Th   F

Amaterasu, p. 786

Directed Reading
- **Reading Level:** Moderate
- **Difficulty Consideration:** Setting
- **Ease Factor:** Sympathetic characters

Pacing
- **Regular Schedule:** 1 day
- **Block Schedule:** 0.5 day

Objectives
Studying this lesson will enable students to
- use reading skills such as drawing conclusions
- define characterization and recognize how it is achieved in the selection
- describe some literary accomplishments of Carolyn Swift
- appreciate a Japanese myth about troubles among the gods

Before Reading

Preview and Motivate
Choose from the following materials to preview the lesson and motivate your students:
____ Before Reading, *SE/ATE*, p. 786
____ Pros and Cons, *Meeting the Standards Unit 8*, p. 72
____ K-W-L Chart, *Meeting the Standards Unit 8*, p. 73

During Reading

Teach the Selection(s)
Choose from the following resources to teach the selection(s):
____ During Reading, *SE/ATE*, pp. 787–790
____ Cultural Connection: Shintoism, *SE/ATE*, p. 789
____ Reading Skills: Identify Text Organization, *SE/ATE*, p. 789
____ Sequence Map, *Meeting the Standards Unit 8*, p. 74

Differentiate Instruction
Consider the following alternative teaching options to differentiate instruction:
____ English Language Learning, *ATE*, p. 788
____ Reading Proficiency, *ATE*, p. 788
____ Auditory and Kinesthetic Learning, *ATE*, p. 790
____ Enrichment, *ATE*, p. 790
____ Reading Strategies and Skills Practice: Take Notes, *Differentiated Instruction for Developing Readers*, pp. 58–60
____ Draw Conclusions, *Differentiated Instruction for English Language Learners*, pp. 200–208

After Reading

Review and Extend
Use the following materials to review and extend the lesson:
____ After Reading, *SE/ATE*, p. 791
____ Myth Writing, *Meeting the Standards Unit 8*, p. 75

Assess

Administer the following assessment tool(s):

____ Selection Quiz, *Meeting the Standards Unit 1,* pp. 76–77

____ Lesson Test, *Assessment Guide,* pp. 239–241

Technology Tools

Enhance the lesson with interactive activities offered in these technology supplements:

- EMC Launchpad
- Annotated Teacher's Edition on CD
- Interactive Student Text on CD
- Exam*View*® Assessment Suite on CD
- Visual Teaching Package
- ETS Online Criterion-Based Essay Grader (Grades 9–12)
- EMC Audio Library
- EMC E-Library
- **mirrorsandwindows.com**

Name: _____ Date: _____

M   T   W   Th   F

Aunty Misery, p. 792

Directed Reading
- **Reading Level:** Easy
- **Difficulty Consideration:** None
- **Ease Factor:** Length and style

Pacing
- **Regular Schedule:** 1 day
- **Block Schedule:** 0.5 day

Objectives
Studying this lesson will enable students to
- use reading skills such as analyzing cause and effect
- define simile and recognize how similes contribute to a story
- name literary accomplishments of Judith Ortiz Cofer and explain how her Puerto Rican heritage influences her writing
- appreciate a folk tale about how misery became a part of life

Before Reading

Preview and Motivate
Choose from the following materials to preview the lesson and motivate your students:
____ Before Reading, *SE/ATE*, p. 792
____ Make Predictions and Creative Writing: Memory Poem, *Meeting the Standards Unit 8*, p. 78

During Reading

Teach the Selection(s)
Choose from the following resources to teach the selection(s):
____ During Reading, *SE/ATE*, pp. 793–794
____ Use Reading Skills: Draw Conclusions, *Meeting the Standards Unit 8*, p. 79

Differentiate Instruction
Consider the following alternative teaching options to differentiate instruction:
____ Enrichment, *ATE*, p. 794
____ Reading Proficiency, *ATE*, p. 794

After Reading

Review and Extend
Use the following materials to review and extend the lesson:
____ After Reading, *SE/ATE*, p. 795
____ Plot Diagram, *Meeting the Standards Unit 8*, p. 80
____ Collaborative Learning: Discuss the Message, *Exceeding the Standards: Extension Activities*, p. 24

Assess
Administer the following assessment tool(s):
____ Selection Quiz, *Meeting the Standards Unit 1*, p. 81
____ Lesson Test, *Assessment Guide*, pp. 242–244

Technology Tools

Enhance the lesson with interactive activities offered in these technology supplements:

- EMC Launchpad
- Annotated Teacher's Edition on CD
- Interactive Student Text on CD
- Exam*View*® Assessment Suite on CD
- Visual Teaching Package
- ETS Online Criterion-Based Essay Grader (Grades 9–12)
- EMC Audio Library
- EMC E-Library
- **mirrorsandwindows.com**

Name: _____ Date: _____

M   T   W   Th   F

The Force of Luck, p. 796

Independent Reading
- **Reading Level:** Easy
- **Difficulty Consideration:** Length
- **Ease Factor:** Simple language and compelling plot

Pacing
- **Regular Schedule:** 2 days
- **Block Schedule:** 1 day

Objectives
Studying this lesson will enable students to
- read with developing fluency
- read silently with comprehension for a sustained period of time

Before Reading

Preview and Motivate
Choose from the following materials to preview the lesson and motivate your students:
_____   Before Reading, *SE/ATE*, p. 796
_____   Practice Vocabulary, *Meeting the Standards Unit 8*, p. 82

During Reading

Teach the Selection(s)
Choose from the following resources to teach the selection(s):
_____   During Reading, *SE/ATE*, pp. 796–802
_____   Reading Skills: Determine Importance of Details, *SE/ATE*, p. 799
_____   Grammar Skills: Compound-Complex Sentences, *SE/ATE*, p. 801
_____   Writing Skills: Thesis Statements, *SE/ATE*, p. 802
_____   Analyze Literature: Folk Tale, *Meeting the Standards Unit 8*, p. 83

Differentiate Instruction
Consider the following alternative teaching options to differentiate instruction:
_____   English Language Learning, *ATE*, p. 798
_____   Reading Proficiency, *ATE*, p. 800
_____   Enrichment, *ATE*, p. 800
_____   Independent Reading Study: The Stories of Rudolfo Anaya, *Differentiated Instruction for Advanced Students*, pp. 49–50

After Reading

Review and Extend
Use the following materials to review and extend the lesson:
_____   After Reading, *SE/ATE*, p. 802
_____   Identify Conflicts, *Meeting the Standards Unit 8*, p. 84
_____   Using Reading Skills: Identify Sequence of Events, *Meeting the Standards Unit 8*, p. 85
_____   Describe and Critique: Folk Literature, *Meeting the Standards Unit 8*, p. 86

Assess

Administer the following assessment tool(s):

_____ Lesson Test, *Assessment Guide*, pp. 245–247

Technology Tools

Enhance the lesson with interactive activities offered in these technology supplements:

- EMC Launchpad
- Annotated Teacher's Edition on CD
- Interactive Student Text on CD
- Exam*View*® Assessment Suite on CD
- Visual Teaching Package
- ETS Online Criterion-Based Essay Grader (Grades 9–12)
- EMC Audio Library
- EMC E-Library
- **mirrorsandwindows.com**

Name: _____ Date: _____

How the Snake Got Poison, p. 803

Independent Reading
- **Reading Level:** Moderate
- **Difficulty Consideration:** Dialect
- **Ease Factor:** Humor

Pacing
- **Regular Schedule:** 1 day
- **Block Schedule:** 0.5 day

Objectives
Studying this lesson will enable students to
- read with developing fluency
- read silently with comprehension for a sustained period of time

---

Before Reading

Preview and Motivate
Choose from the following materials to preview the lesson and motivate your students:
____   Before Reading, *SE/ATE*, p. 803
____   Practice Vocabulary, *Meeting the Standards Unit 8*, p. 89

During Reading

Teach the Selection(s)
Choose from the following resources to teach the selection(s):
____   During Reading, *SE/ATE*, pp. 803–804
____   Analyze Literature: Conflict, *Meeting the Standards Unit 8*, p. 90

After Reading

Review and Extend
Use the following materials to review and extend the lesson:
____   After Reading, *SE/ATE*, p. 804
____   Analyze Literature: Dialect, *Meeting the Standards Unit 8*, p. 91
____   Describe and Critique, *Meeting the Standards Unit 8*, pp. 93–94

Assess
Administer the following assessment tool(s):
____   Selection Quiz, *Meeting the Standards Unit 8*, p. 92
____   Lesson Test, *Assessment Guide*, pp. 248–250

Technology Tools

Enhance the lesson with interactive activities offered in these technology supplements:

- EMC Launchpad
- Annotated Teacher's Edition on CD
- Interactive Student Text on CD
- Exam*View*® Assessment Suite on CD
- Visual Teaching Package
- ETS Online Criterion-Based Essay Grader (Grades 9–12)
- EMC Audio Library
- EMC E-Library
- **mirrorsandwindows.com**

Name: _____ Date: _____

M   T   W   Th   F

Writing Workshop: Expository Writing—Research Report, p. 806

Pacing
- **Regular Schedule:** 3 days
- **Block Schedule:** 1.5 days

Objectives
Participating in this lesson will help enable students to
- write a research report that clearly introduces a purpose and thesis

- write a research report that uses a clear organizational pattern and effective transitions
- support a thesis using quoted, paraphrased, and summarized information from multiple sources
- effectively summarize main points in a conclusion
- write a research report that lists all sources cited

Teach the Workshop

Select from the following resources to teach the workshop:
- _____ Writing Workshop: Expository Writing—Research Report, *SE/ATE*, pp. 806–813
- _____ Writing Skills: Brainstorm, *ATE*, p. 807
- _____ Writing Skills: Avoid Plagiarism, *ATE*, p. 809
- _____ Writing Skills: Predicate Adjectives, *ATE*, p. 811
- _____ Research Skills: Multiple Sources, *ATE*, p. 813
- _____ Language Arts Handbook Section 4.1, The Writing Process, *SE/ATE*, pp. 888–897
- _____ Language Arts Handbook Section 4.2, Modes and Purposes of Writing, *SE/ATE*, p. 897

Differentiate Instruction

Consider the following alternative teaching options to differentiate instruction:
- _____ Kinesthetic Learning, *ATE*, p. 808
- _____ English Language Learning, *ATE*, p. 810
- _____ Reading Proficiency, *ATE*, p. 810

Review and Extend

Use the following materials to review and extend the lesson:
- _____ Narrative Writing: Write a Fable, *Exceeding the Standards: Writing*, pp. 56–64

Technology Tools

Enhance the lesson with interactive activities offered in these technology supplements:
- EMC Launchpad
- Annotated Teacher's Edition on CD
- Interactive Student Text on CD
- Exam*View*® Assessment Suite on CD
- Visual Teaching Package
- ETS Online Criterion-Based Essay Grader (Grades 9–12)
- EMC Audio Library
- EMC E-Library
- **mirrorsandwindows.com**

Name: _____ Date: _____

M T W Th F

Speaking & Listening: Giving and Actively Listening to Research Presentations, p. 814

Pacing
- **Regular Schedule:** 2 days
- **Block Schedule:** 1 day

Objectives
Participating in this lesson will help enable students to
- deliver research presentations that have strong introductions and conclusions
- deliver research presentations that follow clear organization
- deliver research presentations that cover material in depth
- deliver research presentations that support ideas with evidence
- deliver research presentations that incorporate photographs or objects
- deliver research presentations that demonstrate appropriate volume, pacing, eye contact, and nonverbal expression

Teach the Workshop
Select from the following resources to teach the workshop:
____   Speaking & Listening Workshop: Giving and Actively Listening to Research Presentations, *SE/ATE*, pp. 814–815
____   Language Arts Handbook Section 7.1, Verbal and Nonverbal Communication, *SE/ATE*, p. 912
____   Language Arts Handbook Section 7.2, Listening Skills, *SE/ATE*, pp. 913–914
____   Language Arts Handbook Section 7.6, Public Speaking, *SE/ATE*, pp. 916–917

Differentiate Instruction
Consider the following alternative teaching options to differentiate instruction:
____   Reading Proficiency, *ATE*, p. 815

Review and Extend
Use the following materials to review and extend the lesson:
____   Giving and Actively Listening to Research Presentations, *Exceeding the Standards: Speaking & Listening*, pp. 23–25

Technology Tools
Enhance the lesson with interactive activities offered in these technology supplements:
- EMC Launchpad
- Annotated Teacher's Edition on CD
- Interactive Student Text on CD
- Exam*View*® Assessment Suite on CD
- Visual Teaching Package
- ETS Online Criterion-Based Essay Grader (Grades 9–12)
- EMC Audio Library
- EMC E-Library
- **mirrorsandwindows.com**

Name: _____ Date: _____

Test Practice Workshop, p. 816

Pacing
- **Regular Schedule:** 1 day
- **Block Schedule:** 0.5 day

Objectives
Participating in this lesson will help enable students to
- write a research report based on a timed writing prompt

- answer standardized test questions that demonstrate revising and editing skills
- answer standardized questions that demonstrate the ability to make inferences from a reading

Teach the Workshop
Select from the following resources to teach the workshop:

_____ Writing Skills: Research Report, *SE/ATE*, p. 816

_____ Revising and Editing Skills, *SE/ATE*, p. 817

_____ Reading Skills, *SE/ATE*, pp. 818–819

_____ Test-Taking Skills: Choose the Best Answer, *ATE*, p. 819

_____ Language Arts Handbook Section 8.1, Preparing for Tests, *SE/ATE*, p. 921

_____ Language Arts Handbook Section 8.2, Strategies for Taking Standardized Tests, *SE/ATE*, p. 921–922

_____ Language Arts Handbook Section 8.4, Answering Multiple-Choice Questions, *SE/ATE*, p. 922

_____ Language Arts Handbook Section 8.5, Answering Reading Comprehension Questions, *SE/ATE*, p. 923

_____ Language Arts Handbook Section 8.9, Answering Essay Questions, *SE/ATE*, pp. 924–925

_____ Test-Taking Skills and Strategies, *Exceeding the Standards: Test Practice*, pp. 1–4

Differentiate Instruction
Consider the following alternative teaching options to differentiate instruction:

_____ Enrichment, *ATE*, p. 818

_____ English Language Learning, *ATE*, p. 818

Review and Extend
Use the following materials to review and extend the lesson:

_____ Folk Literature Study Guide: Practice Test, *Meeting the Standards Unit 8*, pp. 11–16

_____ SAT Practice Test, *Exceeding the Standards: Test Practice*, pp. 20–23

Technology Tools
Enhance the lesson with interactive activities offered in these technology supplements:

- EMC Launchpad
- Annotated Teacher's Edition on CD
- Interactive Student Text on CD
- Exam*View*® Assessment Suite on CD
- Visual Teaching Package

- ETS Online Criterion-Based Essay Grader (Grades 9–12)
- EMC Audio Library
- EMC E-Library
- **mirrorsandwindows.com**